Brighton's Unsung Heroes

Everyday Lives of Ordinary People

Acknowledgements

Published by QueenSpark Books, a charity which, since 1972, has helped the people of Brighton & Hove to tell their stories.

QueenSpark Books gratefully acknowledges the financial assistance of The National Lottery Heritage Fund, which made possible the Archives Alive project, and Brighton & Hove City Council and the University of Brighton for their ongoing support. With gratitude to all the volunteers and participants in Archives Alive.

Copyright © 2019 QueenSpark Books and the authors and contributors

Brighton's Unsung Heroes – Everyday Lives of Ordinary People

All rights reserved. No part of this publication may be reproduced without written permission, except in the case of brief extracts embodied in articles, reviews or lectures.

First published in Great Britain in 2019 by QueenSpark Books, Brighton, UK.
A catalogue record for this book is available from the British Library
ISBN 978-1-9996699-4-2

Designer Chris Callard www.beachstone.co.uk

Managing Editor John Riches

Developmental Editors Kevin Bacon (Photographs), Evlynn Sharp (Text)

Editors Christina Incorvaja, Robert Jones and Angel Pürschel

Photo Editors Gareth Davies, Ali Ghanimi, Klara Sidoova

Image archives James Gray Collection, QueenSpark Books, Regency Society, Royal Pavilion and Museums, Brighton & Hove

Printed by One Digital, Woodingdean www.one-digital.com

QueenSpark Books
admin@queensparkbooks.org.uk
Web www.queensparkbooks.org.uk
Registered Charity Number 1172938 Company Number 02404473

Copyright disclaimer: Writing and images by kind permission of authors, photographers, and other sources, where possible. QueenSpark Books has made efforts to ensure that the reproduction of content in this publication is done with the full consent of copyright holders. If you feel that your copyright has not been fully respected, please contact us by email: admin@queensparkbooks.org.uk

Contents

Introduction 4

1. Everyday Struggle 7
    Poverty and Lack 8
    Homeless in Brighton 16
    Single Mothers 20

2. Survivors 27
    War 28
    Behind the Front 43

3. Life After Stroke 49
    Life with Stroke 50
    Recovery 52

4. Working Folk 57
    Long Hours 58
    Picket Duty 66
    On the Buses 68
    Someone Has To Do It 71
    On the Sea 76

5. Community 81
    Caring 82
    Trans Brighton 85
    Refuge 86

6. Mr and Mrs Cowley 91
    Harry's Legacy 92
    For a Cause 93
    Labour Man 96
    Harriet Cowley 98

Introduction

Brighton's Unsung Heroes – Everyday Lives of Ordinary People is one of four books produced by QueenSpark Books' volunteers in 2019. It is part of a project to uncover and discover anew the rich and fascinating stories of Brighton and its people using QueenSpark's extensive archives.

Our role in the project was a daunting one – as three volunteer editors to sift through 107 books with no concrete preconception of what we would find. We firstly needed to decide on a theme that would do justice to the treasure trove of stories within QueenSpark's archives, and then to select and compile extracts that would best represent this theme.

Brighton has an absorbing social history and is well known for its diversity. Its various communities and vibrant energy give it a unique identity. But within these communities, it is each individual who makes the city so extraordinary a place. We decided to focus on these 'ordinary' people of Brighton's history, and we came to find innumerable cases of amazing yet perhaps underappreciated individuals worthy of the title unsung hero.

The material from QueenSpark's archives did not disappoint us. Our greatest challenge became not in finding sufficient material but on deciding which extracts to include or to leave out. What settled our decisions in the end was our goal to try our best to limit the book to those accounts that would give as broad, diverse and historically expansive a picture of Brighton's unsung heroes as possible.

Our intention is to give credit to and celebrate ordinary people – and who, at the same time, are exceptionally courageous, persevering, enduring and inspiring each in their own unique ways.

We have given life again to stories that might otherwise be forgotten or ignored. We have included accounts ranging across history: from old to young; from modest to the outright down and out; from leaders to everyday working folk. We wish to give readers of *Brighton's Unsung Heroes* the opportunity to learn about these engaging lives.

Creating this book has been an enjoyable and rewarding experience. We are proud to be a part of the QueenSpark Archives Alive project and to contribute to the continuation of the telling and retelling of accounts. Our hope is readers, too, will find something of value in this book as they gain an intimate insight into the everyday lives, the everyday people, the everyday heroes of Brighton.

Christina Incorvaja, Robert Jones and Angel Pürschel
Editors – *Brighton's Unsung Heroes*

July 2019

CHAPTER 1

Everyday Struggle

A couple sleeping rough in Trafalgar Street, 2011 by Charlotte Leaper.

Poverty and Lack

Bread and margarine . . . .

I couldn't look after myself either on the sixth of March 1930, because that was the day I was born, in Brighton General Hospital, which externally still looks the grim workhouse it had been. I was to be an only child. This was by my mother's choice. Her mother had died whilst she herself was still a child, and to her had fallen the drudgery at the age of 14 of bringing up her two brothers and two of her sisters, one, Hilda, no more than two years old. So by the time she'd married, my mother had already brought up one family, and she'd known the poverty that could go with a brood of children. Sometimes dinner for her had been a slice of bread and margarine, a spread so awful it was known as 'axle grease'. At times my mother served us what to her had been a treat – a dish called 'tombstone' from the moulded shape of the rice mixed with, not milk, but water. To make it appealing, on top went jam, which in her childhood would be bought by the spoonful from the corner shop.

…… **JOHN KNIGHT,**
A HA'P'ORTH OF SWEETS

Brighton General Hospital, 2010 by The Voice of Hassocks.

EVERYDAY STRUGGLE

Charity boots

My mother knew the shame of poverty. Charity boots were given for children in need, and were distinctively marked so the parents couldn't pawn them. My mother beseeched my grandmother not to get her charity boots because she believed that humiliating brand would catch every eye. Because her children's feelings meant more to her than scrimping yet further her mother didn't insist.

JOHN KNIGHT, *A HAP'ORTH OF SWEETS*

Spare ground

Rationing was only part of an austerity campaign attempting to curb civilian consumption, so that scarce resources could be diverted to the war effort. People were exhorted to avoid the 'squander hog', and were advised to collect salvage, to recycle waste, to make do and mend. There were recipes for stretching the rations and making a tasty second meal out of leftovers. When finally unfit for human consumption scraps could be turned into pigswill. People were urged to supplement their rations by 'digging for victory', using any spare ground to grow more food.

MICHAEL CORUM, *BRIGHTON BEHIND THE FRONT*

WW2 Dig for Victory Poster by Peter Fraser. The National Archives.

BRIGHTON'S UNSUNG HEROES

Rag-and-bone man..........................

Not only food was in short supply, clothes were rationed so efforts had to be made to maintain and modify an ever-diminishing wardrobe. The rag-and-bone man became a national hero and people sacrificed their aluminium pots and pans, hoping they would be turned into Spitfires. In this way it was hoped that shipping space would be saved and the German blockade beaten.
..........MICHAEL CORUM, *BRIGHTON BEHIND THE FRONT*

WW2 recyling campaign poster, c.1939-45. The National Archives.

One or two ounces a week............

There wasn't a great deal to recycle, if you bought anything like bottled vinegar, you would take the bottle back and get a new one, or get it filled. No goods were prepackaged other than things like jam, which came in jars (it would be difficult to dole that out). Sugar, lentils, everything like that normally sold by the grocer, after being weighed out, was put into recycled blue paper folded into a sort of twisted cone like an ice cream. The quantities even for a family were very small, because rations tended to be one or two ounces a week. So even if you multiply that for a family of four or five you've got something like ten ounces, a small amount to wrap up. So the basic wrapping was this blue paper, and then of course you used newspaper. If you went to get potatoes, or anything at the greengrocers, you always took along a wicker basket or a small bag, no plastic bags. They put the goods straight into the bag, they didn't wrap vegetables.
..............................BRIAN DUNGATE,
BRIGHTON BEHIND THE FRONT

Help put the lid on Hitler BY SAVING YOUR OLD METAL AND PAPER

EVERYDAY STRUGGLE

Coupons, knitting, recipes.....................

As for clothing, you just made things last, rather than recycled them. There were clothing coupons, you couldn't just go and buy clothes, you had to have the necessary coupons, for example, the few women who got married had to somehow put their wedding outfit together by getting coupons from the family. It meant a great deal of saving and working out what you were going to do. In addition to that, people were adept with their hands, a lot of people knitted. That was certainly recycling, when things which were no longer wanted they were just taken apart and a new garment knitted with the wool. The women's magazines, which were thin and badly printed, recycled paper again, were full of tips on how to unkink the wool when you unpicked it. There were recipes for carrot cake, for sweetening you used saccharine which is revolting... paradoxically people then had a remarkably sweeter tooth than now. People certainly would, if they could, put an immense amount of sweetening in tea or coffee.
..........**BRIAN DUNGATE**, *BRIGHTON BEHIND THE FRONT*

Down a drain................................

I was born on Saturday, 10th September 1898 at 49 Southampton Street, Brighton, Sussex, the third child of Edwin Ernest Parker and Charlotte Grace Parker, née Purser. I remember one occasion when Mum was very hard-up. She sent me to the greengrocers for what she called 'pot-herbs', which was a few carrots, a turnip, or something like that. I never did know why it was called that. She gave me a florin, saying, "Take care," as it was all she had. Well, the inevitable happened. I dropped the precious coin but, being on the hill just below our house, it rolled and went down a drain. I cried, I was so full up. Not that I should be tanned – Mum was not like that. I can't remember what she said, but how did she feel? On one occasion, a postal

BRIGHTON'S UNSUNG HEROES

order for half-a-crown came by post. We never knew where it came from, but Mum always thought it was Aunt Susie – her mother's sister, who lived at 37 Hanover Street. She denied it, but she was a good sort, and I think it was her. Goodness knows, she could not afford it as her husband was an invalid for years – I think it was Bright's disease. Anyway, that's real unsung kindness, isn't it?

.... GEORGE PARKER, *THE TALE OF A BOY SOLDIER*

Parish Relief..

It must be remembered that there was no unemployment pay then. One could only apply for Parish Relief, a very degrading thing, if one had any pride. A ticket would be issued only if you could prove that you were really destitute. This was a slip of paper with a few absolute necessities printed on it, and the shops were forbidden to supply anything which was not on the list. The amount varied, but was mostly under ten shillings.

> 'I knew what poverty was, so I would break the rules and let them have it'

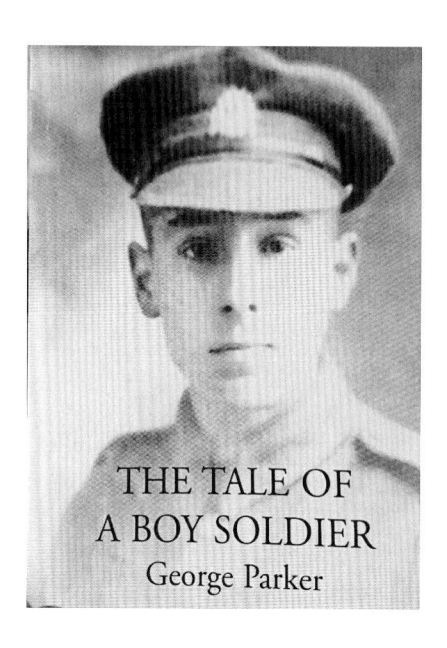

I have had poor women come in the shop and beg me to let them have a little tobacco for their husbands, instead of sugar; she would do without it in her tea, only her man had not had a smoke for so long. What could I do? I knew what poverty was, so I would break the rules and let them have it. Yes, those were Dickensian days all right. The Parish also had soup kitchens in Cobden Road, where the very poor could

George Parker,
The Tale of a Boy Soldier,
QueenSpark Books.

THE TALE OF A BOY SOLDIER
George Parker

EVERYDAY STRUGGLE

get soup for tuppence a quart. I have been there many times with a washstand jug to get a gallon for our dinner. It cost eightpence. It was quite good soup or seemed like it to us, who were hungry. The London Road Congregational Church had a blanket society which would lend out blankets to the poor for the winter, for a very small sum, provided they were returned clean at the end. Emmie and I used to go for some blankets each winter to a Mr Hamilton in Wellington Road.

.... GEORGE PARKER, *THE TALE OF A BOY SOLDIER*

Three pounds a week ....

We did enjoy life. It was no good being miserable. You can't live, and cut yourself off. If you've got friends, you've got to join in – so, we all had a good laugh. It was all we could do really. We had nothing else to enjoy, so we used to go out and enjoy ourselves.

But, you couldn't go out every night because the money wouldn't run to it. And the point was you couldn't go out for a long time because the buses stopped running at nine o'clock. So, if you didn't catch the bus home you had to walk, and more often than not it was dark. We would start out – four or five of us – and gradually, one left, then another, and finally you were on your own.

Back to work after baby: in 1949 my husband was earning just over three pounds a week and that was good money in those days. At the time, my father didn't earn as much. You didn't pay a lot of rent, but, then, we had the baby to think of and we had nobody to give us anything.

A pram was fifteen pounds and a cot seven and we had to start from scratch. Now, they have credit cards, but then, if you hadn't got the money you couldn't have the goods, unless you used such things as Co-op cheques. So to build up our living wage, as you

> **'If you've got friends, you've got to join in'**

might say, I went back to work after the baby arrived. It wasn't a recognised thing in those days for a woman to go out to work. But, I did go back.

.................................JOAN PARSONS, *JOBS FOR LIFE*

Poor Law

I was born, one of twins, on the 22nd January, 1905. My father was a carpenter and by 1913 we were in a dire position. My mother had died when I was five years old and there was no work about. Men were walking the streets, led by a band and going about begging for pennies to keep themselves going. My father was out of work for a very long time and we had to go to the Poor Law to get coupons for the necessities of life. I used to queue up at the Corporation Soup Kitchen with a big jug, like you used to have in bedrooms and get it filled up with really delicious hot soup for a penny. Although they thought they were giving us all the old rubbish that was thrown away by the tradespeople – the odds and ends that came off carcasses for instance – it was really good and nutritious. I remember one day in particular, I was wearing boots given to me by the school (we used to walk about barefooted from the spring to the late autumn, not because we liked it, but because we couldn't buy boots). I went as usual with my jug and waited two or three hours for the soup to be cooked and when I came out with my jug full of boiling soup, I slipped down and poured it all over my head. In those days our families weren't educated in how to deal with an accident and my older sister poured oil over it and it was terrifying. I had a dreadful head as a result of that. My head was covered with a bandage and every night my father used to get a bowl of water, soak the bandage and take it off. The last part was stuck and he used to say, "Hold tight!" and snatch it off.

Also in those days, because people had nothing – nothing at all – you never knew when your next-door neighbour was going

> 'You would suddenly find that a neighbour two doors away had drowned themselves or thrown themselves over the cliffs because the burden of life was intolerable'

to commit suicide. People would be unable to pay their rent, which would only be five shillings for a house, and that shared with two or three families, living in slum conditions, not dirty, but crowded because there was not enough money. You would suddenly find that a neighbour two doors away had drowned themselves or thrown themselves over the cliffs because the burden of life was intolerable, and that was at a time when you could buy a newspaper for a halfpenny.
........................JOHN LANGLEY, *ALWAYS A LAYMAN*

First Aid

I started in a First Aid class at the railway when I was 14 years old. The doctor who lectured spoke very quietly and when it came to bleeding I could see it all happening, so I fainted along with four policemen who trained with us. It was because of listening so intently. I spent many years on First Aid and then it led me into becoming a Blood Donor. I gave 43 donations, then they wouldn't take any more because of my age. One of the things my aunt used to say was, "Never have any fear of illness or diseases, don't be afraid to mix with people who have infectious diseases and help them when you can. You would never have doctors and nurses if they were afraid." I have always lived that way. When I was young T.B. was rife (poverty again), and we were forbidden to mix. Death was inevitable, but I always mixed and was never afraid. Today it does not mean a thing due to progress in treatment and a better start in life which all children get. They look wonderful today. Where we had fear, they have confidence.
.... JOHN LANGLEY, *ALWAYS A LAYMAN*

John Langley, *Always a Layman*, QueenSpark Books.

BRIGHTON'S UNSUNG HEROES

Homeless in Brighton

Anonymous lives . . . .
For the most part, the homeless lead anonymous lives; they are used to the eyes of passers-by slipping away from them. Their circumstances place them within a category: street people, addicts, service users. They are seldom regarded as anything else; we know little of their personalities, imaginations or desires.
. . . . *ROOFLESS*

Lonely years . . . .
Looking back, I wonder why I could not show my feelings; to love and be loved. I would give anything if I could turn the clock back and show you the real me without the drink and drugs. After so many lonely years, with you and the kids always in my thoughts and prayers, I cringe at some of the things I said and did under the influence of drink; the insanity of loving drink more than you – the times that I walked out to get a drink leaving you crying, begging me to come back.

I have spent many lonely nights longing to tell you how sorry I have been, to hold you, look into your eyes and

Homeless in Brighton, 2019 by Klara Sidoova.

EVERYDAY STRUGGLE

say, "I love you." I guess it's only words, and actions speak louder than words. That's why I just stay out of your life. Maybe I am afraid to see you again, afraid to bring out all of the emotions and feelings that I have buried deep down in my heart. Yes, I have changed. I only wish I could give you all the real love I have learned since I last saw you. Growing up is hard to do. I wish you all the happiness on your journey through life. I guess I had to lose you to find me. You will always have a special place in my heart. I have learned so much from you. As I get to understand the meaning of love, I love you more each day. Today I can only let go, and let God and I feel privileged for you being there as part of my journey.
.... DANNY, *ROOFLESS*

> '**As I get to understand the meaning of love, I love you more each day**'

The whole story..............................

People have often asked me, "Why did you become homeless?" To say it was just because of the drink or drugs, although they are a major factor, is not the whole story. There is a total lack of responsibility, a freedom, a camaraderie and an adrenalin-fuelled survival buzz which is as liberating as it is nihilistic, that fulfils some kind of primal need within me.

Society gives us the rules to live by, but when you're homeless, most of those rules go by the board. Why? Because, if your homelessness is based upon a need to drink, to acquire and use the money to do so, there are no rules, except – 'don't get caught'.

You may be dependent upon your drug of choice, but, once the need is met, you can start to enjoy the superficial temporal freedoms it gives you. It has always struck me as funny that the people who tell you to get a life and get a job are usually unhappy with their own. So pass the bottle Danny.
.... DANNY, *ROOFLESS*

BRIGHTON'S UNSUNG HEROES

One more quick call.........................

It was a hot, sunny day and I was feeling sweaty and quite weak by the time I had brokered a heroin deal. I could now smell vomit mixed with the more pungent urea and was glad to have only one more quick call to make. The crack dealer sounded short, sharp and angry when I finally spoke. "Who is dis?" he was saying. "Me," I said. I had been retching and sneezing when he answered.

Within the hour, I had connected and walked home with both parcels. The brown one on its own would have been OK, maybe. The white one with it spelled disaster really, but still I couldn't see this, however many times it happened. I could forget the historic and probable outcome of Paul smoking crack.

Homeless in Brighton, 2019 by Klara Sidoova.

In my room at the hostel I lived like a prisoner – a small, narrow, corridor-like space, a bed, a wardrobe, sounds, TV, too much stuff all crammed into too small a space. It was like a strange tribal dance trying to navigate in one direction from door to bed, collecting up my pipe and paraphernalia on the way.

EVERYDAY STRUGGLE

Within minutes my room now felt like Vietnam. The crack had me feeling as though I was under attack, surveillance and suspicion. A war zone erupted in my mind and the compulsion to look under the door was now too strong to resist.

If anyone was watching me, they'd have been in hysterics. All I could do was tiptoe about, lay down flat and see if anyone was outside my door, twitch curtains and hold my breath so I could hear them, whoever they were. This didn't reflect my business plan of getting out and about to serve up other brownheads and make my money back... On my first telephone order I went down to the town centre. It turned out to be a bit of a turkey and my friend claimed to have got confused. We decided to stroll to another phone box, probably a stinker, to order another crack rock. Not good.

This is where my destiny was underlined. Whilst leaving the house I saw a police car. My decision-making process was f*****. Instead of leaving the gear at the house, I thought we may see some punters en route. The only people I saw were the same police, who were armed and decided to stop and search me. The rest is obvious, only I didn't miss my rehab placement. I was tried, found guilty and given a six-month bail date to return for sentencing.

I made the significant changes to my life that the courts so rarely see and am writing this a free man in every sense of the word.
.... PAUL, *ROOFLESS*

> '**I made the significant changes to my life that the courts so rarely see**'

Single Mothers

> 'I feel that being a parent in this society is a perilous business'

Silent and unseen ....

My mother (who should be in Parliament) tells me to, "Get a job." She tells me that I ought to be grateful for the welfare state, which she spent her working life putting into. Some people, she says, never know the back of poverty, dependence, ill health and illiteracy. I chose to keep the baby, so I've got to pull myself up by the boot-straps. Mother, I want to tell you something. I unfailingly provide 24-hour care to the best of my abilities for my little boy. The trap that I live in is silent and unseen until one has fallen in. I can't get a part-time job because I'd be simply paying for the child-care while I'm working. I'd need a full-time job which pays £300 a week to be able to save anything. I live a gnawing tedium of juggling with so-called options when all I really juggle with is thin air. Yes, I chose to have a baby, but why punish me now that it's too late?

At various times and for various reasons I've felt all the things society and the Government says I am. I've felt irresponsible and naive, lacking in authority, emotionally screwed-up and insensitive to my son and the rest of the world; I've felt like a scrounger who's only ever taken from the welfare state, scruffy and grubby in an uncaring way, especially in the Children's Library and at nursery.

I don't however worry about being 'socially dangerous' because I see through that pitiful veneer of political manoeuvring. Nonetheless I often worry about my son growing up to be 'out of control', becoming a physically huge fifteen-year-old who answers back and enjoys petty crime, hard drugs and violent bullying! I fear that future so much. Will my son be disadvantaged

EVERYDAY STRUGGLE

like society says he will? All of these feelings show my own insecurities as a person and as a parent. I feel that being a parent in this society is a perilous business. I walk about seeing looks on people's faces and I hear that tone in their voice and I wonder how much of it is true vibe and how much is paranoia. Paranoia stemming from my expectations and judgments of myself. I hear society hissing that I'm right to feel bad about myself.
....LIZ, *THE LONE RANGERS*

Prejudice..................................

More obvious, overt prejudice that I receive has been more connected to the fact that my son is mixed-race rather than the fact that I'm single, although through caring for a mixed-race child I've found that one is almost expected to be single, even by other parents of mixed-race children. When I had my first scan at the hospital the nurse called, "Mrs R?" I panicked and thought, "Shit, my mother's come down on a surprise visit!" I immediately realised that the nurse was calling me. I called across to her and told her that. "I am not Mrs R. That is my mother. I am Miss R." I felt crushed by indignation. The nurse laughed and said that she was always marrying people off. It hadn't occurred to me before that someone would make an assumption about the prefix to your name. Since then I've learned to expect this. Actually, unless it's necessary I don't

The Lone Rangers, **QueenSpark Books.**

correct the mistake. I think that I secretly enjoy the respect that having married woman status brings. It means that you are talked to eye to eye, rather than eye to top of head. It means that you are allowed to be assertive, ask lots of questions, be a grown-up. It means you can handle money, that you know about the secrets of men, that you are in society. It means that you are acceptable.

I know that I've been warned against letting my son sleep next to me. I know too that he, being two years old, must not be expected to be a crutch for my emotional screw-ups. But the other night, after being told that I was 'redundant' (meant I'm sure in a humorous, "Look at me, I'm coping," kind of way) by my son's father who'd spent one night looking after his child, I began to cry. I felt so crap as a mother. So tired, so angry at the inequality, so scared of my responsibility, too helpless to fight. My child was asleep but he turned over and kissed my eyes. I cried harder then but for different reasons.
....LIZ, *THE LONE RANGERS*

Squalid living conditions......................

When Joe was a baby I did an intensive conversion course, which gave me an MSc in Information Systems – which was supposed to get me a well-paid job. I didn't get one for various reasons – a mixture of me, the state of the local and national economies and fortune. So although I have computing and other various skills to offer – secretarial, administrative, TEFL teaching – I'm on Income Support and have been for the last two years.

This makes me angry. I could have signed on at one of the temp agencies to do secretarial work or taught in a language school in the holidays. Why not? Because none of this would have paid enough to cover rent, childminding, bills, food and tax. Far from it. And because – even if those jobs did pay enough – they are

EVERYDAY STRUGGLE

by nature temporary and coming back on Income Support and getting your rent paid by Housing Benefit again takes months. Meanwhile, you're out on the streets. Many two-wage-earner families struggle to raise children these days. I shouldn't be surprised that I can't afford to earn my own living.

We've just moved. We've moved three times since Joe was born – that's every year of his life so far. And I don't expect things to change. At the moment, we're lucky. Our last move was from a damp, one-bedroom flat to a house with two bedrooms and a garden. Joe loves it here and that's good, but it's difficult to encourage him to enjoy it and feel at home because in ten months' time we might well have to move again. When you're on Income Support and totally reliant on the combination of high private-sector rents and Housing Benefit, you really have no control over where you live and for how long. Joe might well grow up with no concept of 'home' at all, just a series of places where we've lived. As if all this wasn't enough to unnerve and unsettle us, threats to reduce Housing Benefit to force people like us into squalid living conditions mean that Joe's future 'homes' could be very bleak ones indeed.
.............................**SHIRLEY**, *THE LONE RANGERS*

> '**I don't expect things to change**'

I love it ....
Laden with shopping, bum at right-angles, I squeak and click the pram up the hill to our café treat. They know us now and pass me two menus as my sweat breaks out in sweat and I curse the unfoldable folding pram. The two of us sit on high chairs and ponder the inevitable on the menu. From here a big grown-up game starts. My son runs his fingers down the list going, "Mmmm?" and orders chocolate milkshake. I add one for myself and an emergency waffle with chocolate sauce and whipped cream, just in case.

We sit and wait, the child occasionally shouting, "Where's milkshake?" We watch the world of cool and vibe passing by. He points out funny hats, orange wheels, big birds, someone looking out of a window, a large van squeezing by, a crying baby, clouds drifting, rain coming, umbrellas clashing, dogs weeing. He giggles at the plant getting up my nose. We act like co-conspirators, plotting. He makes a play for the salt and pepper but the milkshakes arrive just in time. We sip quietly until an inch or so into the drinks when he starts blowing. It's quiet at first; all I know of his game is the sudden splash of chocolate wet in my face and the memory of nearly but not quite packing the damn flannel. I make a half-hearted attempt at stopping him, but really it's quite funny and I'm more interested in watching the milk bubbles grow ever larger around the top of the glass. We solemnly eat the hot waffle. He digs his fingers into the cream and noisily announces that, "It's delicious." The people in the café are dying with delight and my son knows it: he's showing off and I love it.
..................................**LIZ**, *THE LONE RANGERS*

> 'Learning about her… the most exciting and fulfilling time of my life'

Discovery..

Before I had Bethan I had decided that I would never have any children – I had seen what it had done to my two sisters and decided that I would never be like that; the bags under the eyes, the sharp tone of voice and quick to anger. That wasn't for me, I was going to stay a member of the human race and enjoy my life. Do exactly as I pleased when I pleased.

When Bethan came along it was a voyage of discovery. Learning about her and the way she has learned and developed has been the most exciting and fulfilling time of my life.
..............................**DAWN**, *THE LONE RANGERS*

EVERYDAY STRUGGLE

The Lone Rangers,
QueenSpark Books.

CHAPTER TWO

Survivors

Bomb damage in Richmond St, Albion Hill area, 1940s. The James Gray Collection.

War

Daylight raids

The Lewes Road Inn, at the bottom of Franklin Road, was bombed and one of the barmaids was killed. And part of our roof came down. My mother had been to the shop, came back, and just managed to get under the steps. The top of our roof came down and just missed her. There was another hit on a house at the top of Caledonian Road and everyone died including a new-born baby. These were daylight raids. Whether we were hit by a bomb or a shell from a gun we didn't know. But, a pilot may have been on his way back and dropped his bombs to lose weight.

JOAN PARSONS, *JOBS FOR LIFE*

Defence preparations at Palace Pier, Brighton, c.1940. Royal Pavilion and Museums.

Run home

Another day we were running home from East Brighton Park as the planes were coming over. The soldiers at the anti-aircraft gun shouted to us to get into their tent, one soldier lay over our heads and told us to put our fingers in our ears. The gun fired at the German planes, but thanks to that soldier, my hearing and life are still intact fifty years later. We were then told to run home.

EILEEN ANDERSON, *BRIGHTON BEHIND THE FRONT*

A normal day

In 1943 the most memorable thing in my whole life occurred. It was the nearest to death I had ever come. It started off as a

SURVIVORS

normal day and the routine in the shop was unchanged. It was quite a pleasant day really and I was feeling on top of the world as I re-arranged the uncovered bacon rashers before me. The sirens had sounded minutes earlier and as usual we took no notice of them. The shop was empty of customers. We heard the planes droning overhead and disregarded them also, until we heard the scream of the bomb falling.

Just as though we were all tethered to the same strand of elastic, and a hidden hand gave it a yank, as one person, we all made a mad dash to the rear of the shop. For what purpose, I have no idea, except that we all thought there was safety at the top of the cellar stairs. The only real safety would have been from flying glass. Anyway, the back of the shop was as far as we got.

Air raid damage to the London Road viaduct, 1944.

'I can still feel the impact of the blast on my chest'

The explosion that followed was tremendous, and to this day I can still feel the impact of the blast on my chest. A roar and shattering of glass followed instantaneously. We huddled together and it seemed like an eternity before anyone dared to move. The air was full of choking dust, and as everything subsided back to normality, we very shakily ventured back to the main part of the shop. Our legs felt as though they consisted of nothing but jelly. A lot of the female staff were near to hysteria and tears ran down their faces.

We viewed the destruction with horrified eyes. The shop windows had imploded leaving us open to the elements. The bacon rashers, under their covering of dust, were speared with splinters of glass and nearly everything had blown free from the shelves. As I made my way to the shop door, I noticed cans of food rolling across the pavement into the gutter. Across the road, there was a gaping hole in the viaduct, and a few soldiers were emerging from the old school building.

The air was still thick with dust as the rubble subsided into an ungainly heap. Our branch of the International was licensed to sell wines and spirits, and Molly Mitchell made her way to the fixtures that held these expensive items. Amidst the carnage and destruction, it was unbelievable to find that these bottles remained intact. She sent the apprentice to the cellar to bring up some clean cups. She emphasized the word 'clean' and she removed a bottle of brandy from the shelf. The apprentice was

A span of the Preston Road viaduct destroyed in one of Brighton's worst raids on 25 May, 1943. Royal Pavilion & Museums.

SURVIVORS

a little reluctant to go. I am sure he thought the shop was going to collapse on top of him, but he decided to go rather than let anyone think he was scared.

With the cups now assembled before her on a hastily-wiped counter, she opened the bottle and gave us all a drink, which she insisted that we all consume. Then she went to the entrance and called to the soldiers to come across. They were a lot more shaken up than us because they had been a lot nearer to the explosion. They shambled slowly across, supporting one of their comrades who had blood pouring down his face. They were really grateful for the brandy. Then Molly Mitchell took the Canadian soldier up to her flat and gave him simple first-aid by placing a plaster over the nasty gash above his eye. The Canadian soldiers had been doing a course in the school building when the bomb came down.

One very important question remained to be asked. How was the empty bottle of brandy going to be explained away to head office? Molly Mitchell had the answer to that as, without hesitation, she promptly smashed the bottle and threw it down amongst the debris waiting to be cleared up ...

As a matter of interest, many years after the war was over, the Canadian soldier who had been cut over the eye, made a pilgrimage back to the shop. He looked such a different person in civilian clothes. He was very sad at not

'They were really grateful for the brandy'

Staff at the International Stores, *International Service*, QueenSpark Books.

being able to see Molly Mitchell, because for years he had always remembered her kindness to him on the day of the bomb. He had now lost the sight in his eye. I could not fix up a date for him to meet her because he was leaving England later that evening.
.... **KATHLEEN WILSON,** *INTERNATIONAL SERVICE*

Among the debris ....

There was no warning – it came like a thunderbolt. I don't think I heard anything. As I was thrown to the ground, I do remember, however, seeing the fascia board of the shop shattering and the bits flying, and being enveloped in dust. The cause was one of the bombs dropped in Albion Hill and Dinapore Street by a German warplane. As I lay among the debris from the fascia board and the glass from the big shop window, there came the sound of running metal-shod boots. It was from soldiers who were training in the Congregational Church hall at the top of the street. I must have told them where I lived, because they took me there. The front door having been blasted open, they laid me in our passage, on the run of carpet. I asked for, and got, a glass of water. For some odd reason I wanted to turn it upside-down on the floor, but someone gently stopped me. I was driven to the hospital by a curate from St Peter's, in his car, laid along the back seat. I was ten years old.

In the ward after I'd arrived at the hospital, I lay isolated behind screens. Excited voices of two little boys playing, reached me. A young nurse said, "Shush, a little boy is dying behind those screens." I would like to say along with Douglas Bader when he heard a similar remark and went on to fly fighters again with tin legs, that writing me off like that made me determined to prove her wrong. Truth is I wasn't concerned one way or the other. Just one thing had bothered me. It was the smell – a smell I could recall for years afterwards, sweetish – on my skin from the

> '**Writing me off like that made me determined to prove her wrong**'

SURVIVORS

explosion. An understanding sister had told two nurses to wash me, but carefully.

It was so appropriate that the one to give blood for a transfusion for me was my Uncle Bill. Among my uncles he was the favourite, firstly because he was a giver. He'd given me money or bought me sweets or an ice-cream whenever we met him. Once it was a bucket and spade, which made me cry because when I filled the bucket with sea-water it slowly leaked away. I wasn't really consoled after a repair had been made with plasticine. Also my uncle was a favourite because on seeing his youngest brother,

Clean up work at a bomb damaged house in the Albion Hill area of Brighton, c.1941. Royal Pavilion & Museums.

sister-in-law and nephew, he beamed. His generosity didn't come from wealth as his home was on the council estate at Whitehawk and he was employed at Brighton Station on the platform staff, a job he did with pride, being official but not officious, standing short in his uniform, his face round and rosy, his head with hardly a hair on top covered by his big uniform hat. My Aunt Rose, his wife, was darkly continental of hair and eyes as she was originally Belgian. She had met my uncle during the First World War, not in Belgium but in England where she was a refugee. To her fell the task of keeping my uncle's generosity within bounds.
.... **JOHN KNIGHT**, *A HA'P'ORTH OF SWEETS*

Unforgettable ....

Sydney Lawrence was born in 1917 at number 54 Waterloo St., which is still there. It was one of the first streets in Hove. He said, with a laugh, "My dad was away fighting in France and he came home on leave. I reckon I was the result!" A sister was born later in 1920.

He went to Middle St. School until he won a scholarship to Patcham High School for Boys, where he attended until he was 16. Then he was apprenticed to Rayners, the opticians, who had a factory in Kemptown. In his late teens he studied optics at the Polytechnic in London... now City College, and he qualified as an optician in 1939. Quite a break away from the trade of his father, who was a self-employed bespoke tailor, working from home.

In 1938 Sydney joined the RAF Voluntary Reserve, so was one of the first to be conscripted in September 1939, as an instrument engineer and navigator with 5th Bomber Command.

He was involved in the earliest raids of the war on Germany in 106 squadron, flying Hampden's Light bombers with a five-man

> 'I was determined to be one of those survivors'

SURVIVORS

crew. "I was determined to be one of those survivors so I tried to learn their language and managed to build up a kind of rapport with some of our jailers who were more amenable. I was moved around to different camps to supplement the work force, until, in January 1945, I was working for Mitsubishi in Nagasaki."

He then went on to recall that fateful day on 9th August 1945. "It was a beautiful morning and I was working near a heap of rubble... the result of bombing by the Allies. At around 11.00am I saw three large planes flying in formation. The two outside ones peeled off, then the centre one circled – and dropped its load... the PLUTONIUM BOMB!"

His voice shook as he continued, "I saw a flash. Then huge columns of smoke rose up. I stood paralysed behind the mountain of rubble, unable to move – or think! I saw people who were now dust swirling around, with their shadows still emblazoned on the ground... dead dust, but evidence of their existence still there to see! Ugh!... Unforgettable!"

I was surprised that he hadn't been affected by the blast. He went on, "Well, you see, the side of anything that faced the impact was blasted to bits, but the sheltered side was left more or less untouched. Trees were pure white on one side where the flash had struck, yet the other side still had green leaves on. Where I was crouching was untouched, yet the other side of the mound was flattened by the blast. Of

Mushroom cloud after nuclear bomb exploded over Nagasaki on 9 August 1945. U.S. National Archives and Records Administration.

the 2,000 Allies there, only half survived the initial impact, but many more died afterwards. As I stood amongst the 85,000 dead inhabitants, I asked myself... 'Why not me?' I felt guilty at being left alive. And the horror of it all was so pointless. When the war with Japan finished on 16th August the Americans dropped food parcels and the surviving POWs helped the sick and dying people... the Jap guards just disappeared. A couple of weeks later the US troops landed and took us to Okinawa in the Philippines, where we were isolated in hospital. Some died there and the rest of us were taken to Manila and Sydney, and eventually, those certified fit enough were landed back in England for Christmas 1945."

> 'I felt guilty at being left alive'

After the war, Sydney went back to optics, married a local girl in 1948 and a son was born in 1949. I asked him whether he had suffered any effects from the radiation. He said, "We knew little of the long-term, genetic effects in those days, but when my wife was pregnant, I spent 24 hours a day praying that the child would be OK, and not have some kind of mutation! Even now," he went on, "I still get nightmares. I still get guilt feelings that I was saved. Yes, I do have to cover up in the sun, otherwise I get a horrible rash. Every day I thank God, when I see my son, now 43, and my two grandchildren, that they have not suffered any radiation or genetic effects."

Sydney retired 10 years ago and his wife died shortly after. Now he lives alone with his memories, alleviated only by the times he sees his family and friends.
........SYDNEY LAWRENCE, *WE'RE NOT ALL ROTHSCHILDS!*

A Mixed Lot ....

Inside the office there was a Recruiting Sergeant and an Officer, as well as a Medical Officer. I was really scared, but the Sergeant asked me what I wanted, I looked so young. Then I said that I wanted to join up, and he looked at me as if I should still be in my cradle. I suppose he was not far wrong! He asked my age and I boldly said, "18 years." He looked at me with a smile and asked, "Does your mother know that you are 18?" Then he said, "All right, son, 18 it is." He took my name, and passed me over to the MO who had me strip naked, examined and passed me. The Officer then made me take the Oath of Allegiance and there I was, a soldier at 15¾.

A recruit was given one shilling on joining – one day's pay – known as taking the King's shilling. They told me that I should get my call-up in due course. In fact, it was over six months, owing to my age, I expect. It's queer, as I think of it now, how impatient I was, daft little idiot!

After another roll call, we were marched through some streets to what looked like a large open space, all dry sand. There seemed to be miles of it, somewhere behind the harbour. We took over a large camp where the tents had been vacated by some poor baskets who had moved on to warmer climes. What a mixed lot there were from various units, including Highlanders who sat on the sand, moaning because, believe it or not, they did not wear anything under the kilt and all their lower parts were smothered in sand!

While we were there, a fellow scraped about in the sand in his tent and there was an old Mills grenade buried underneath. The pin must have rusted away and he blew himself, an officer and four other men to pieces. Killed without even seeing the fighting. Queer how fate works things out for some of us.
.... GEORGE PARKER, *THE TALE OF A BOY SOLDIER*

> 'It's queer, as I think of it now, how impatient I was'

> 'I suppose we were like the ostrich, buried our heads in the sand and hoped for the best'

Shrapnel ....

My first time up the line lasted two weeks. Then those who lived to do so, struggled out under fire to a spot a mile or two behind the line for a so-called rest. This was supposed to be a week during which we scraped some of the mud off us, deloused ourselves as much as possible and got ready to go through it all again. Often though, if the troops who took over from us had a bad time with the loss of many men, back into the line we had to go, even if we had only been out for a day. Of course, it couldn't be helped but it was a dreadful strain.

Rations were a problem too. Often the ration wagons, which were mostly horse-drawn at that time, were wiped out on the journey. The only way we would know was when no food turned up. It was only horseflesh cut into squares and put in sandbags and one loaf between three men, but it just kept us alive. If it was not there for a day or two, bad as it was, you missed it. The meat used to be covered in hairs from the sandbags and they had to be scraped off before it could be eaten. It shows what you will eat if half-starved. Sometimes it would be a 12oz tin of bully beef between three. As a treat, a tin of lemon marmalade came up. Always lemon, I don't know why. I have never liked lemon marmalade any more to this day.

Our part of the trench was at intervals strafed by quick-firing guns. The reports of the guns and the shells from them were so close together that they were known as whizzbangs. Everything the Germans did was methodical. The spells of shelling came at such regular intervals that you could have set your watch by them. Anyway, all one could do was crouch down under what was dignified by the name of dugout, which was usually an odd scrap of corrugated iron scrounged from somewhere, with a few sandbags on top, laid over a hole laboriously cut out of the back of the trench. Of course, it was only protection against flying

SURVIVORS

pieces of shell casing or shrapnel. A direct hit and we would have had it. I suppose we were like the ostrich, buried our heads in the sand and hoped for the best!

I was last wounded on 17th October 1918, during the middle or the end of one of the toughest spots I had been in with the Sherwoods. This was my last action in a battle of World War One and ended my active service career.
.... GEORGE PARKER, *THE TALE OF A BOY SOLDIER*

First time home..............................

I, with a few chaps who were going my way, left the Palace at about 1.00am and caught one of the extra trains to Victoria Station running for troops going home, then the train to Brighton. The first time home for ten months.

Hanover Terrace, c.1970. Royal Pavilion & Museums.

I arrived at 74 Hanover Terrace at 2.30am. Of course, they were all asleep. Selfishly, I suppose, I knocked and knocked, until Dad's voice called to know who was there. I shouted through the letterbox, "It's George!" Mum and Dad tumbled out of bed, down the stairs, and what a welcome I had. Poor old Mum said, "I am so very glad you are safe," and hugged me. Dad was not usually one to show his feelings, but even he was nearly in tears. Yes, it's nice to be wanted! We were all drinking tea for a couple of hours before trying to get a bit of sleep. Then, in the bedroom my brothers wanted to know about my adventures, so I doubt whether we had much rest... In front now, was the settling down to civilian life as a man.

.... GEORGE PARKER, *THE TALE OF A BOY SOLDIER*

Indian Soldiers..................................

The Royal Pavilion was converted into an Indian Hospital and a great many Indian soldiers were treated for their wounds. A great many died of their wounds. Their bodies were taken on to the hills of Patcham and cremated. This spot is known as The Chattri. All around the Pavilion were ornamental iron railings (now gone) and fixed to these was a closely boarded wooden fence about 8 feet high (for privacy), to stop the general public from peering in.

As some of the Indian soldiers got better of their wounds (a good many had arms and legs amputated) they wanted a little more freedom and so it became a familiar sight to see a crutch flung over the high fence and then another crutch, followed by an Indian soldier with one leg scrambling over the high fence. He would gather up his crutches quickly and off he would go (probably to visit some friends he had made or to a hideaway club to have a sly drink).

I would like to add, that all wounded soldiers (British or Indian) were dressed in blue (coat and trousers) and also they all wore red ties. The reason being that they were not allowed inside public houses and served with drinks. Any publicans found serving beer to any wounded soldier were heavily fined and also liable to have their licences taken away.

> 'We were ... taken into the hospital wards and received a great welcome from the wounded Indian soldiers'

SURVIVORS

Us schoolchildren were all lined up in our playground and then marched four-deep through various streets, down to the Indian Hospital. The large iron gates were opened and we all marched. We were met by a military guide and taken into the hospital wards and received a great welcome from the wounded Indian soldiers, some very badly wounded, others sitting up in their beds and a good many pushing themselves around in wheelchairs. We gave them some sweets and cigarettes. From the wards we were taken to the operating theatre and met some of the doctors who kindly explained to us some of the various implements and gas cylinders, etc. From here we were taken to the kitchens and as we passed through we were given a round flat piece of pastry (all nicely baked and rich brown). This was called chu-pattie, or Indian bread. We were very proud of this, also our visit to the Indian Hospital.

And so out into the fresh air once again. Open came the large gates again and home we went, excitedly carrying our round of Indian bread to show our parents and friends. When we arrived back at school the next morning us children had a shock, because we all had to write a composition of our visit to the Indian Hospital and so we had to recall our memories of what we saw. But apart from this, it was a wonderful experience that I have never forgotten.

The dedication and unveiling ceremony of the Indian Memorial Gateway, 26 Oct 1921.
Royal Pavilion & Museums.

BRIGHTON'S UNSUNG HEROES

After the 1914-1918 war came to an end the Indian Government were so thankful to the inhabitants of Brighton for the hospitality we gave to their wounded soldiers that they had built (at their own expense) a great magnificent gateway (at the south end). Carved into the stonework on one side of the gateway are these words:

THIS GATEWAY IS THE GIFT OF INDIA IN COMMEMORATION OF HER SONS WHO STRICKEN IN THE GREAT WAR WERE TENDED IN THE PAVILION IN 1914 AND 1915.

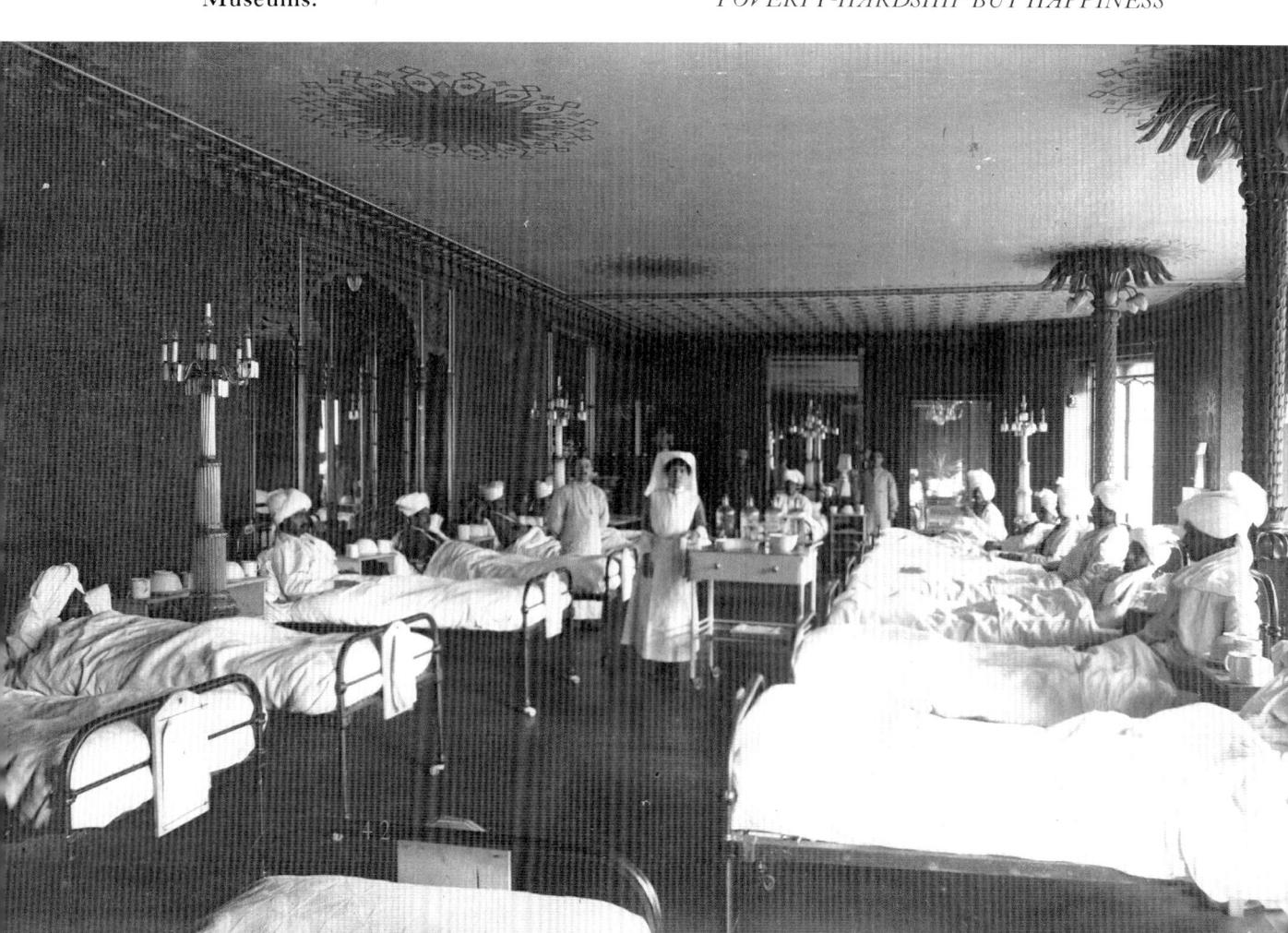

.... ALBERT SYDNEY PAUL,
POVERTY-HARDSHIP BUT HAPPINESS

Indian Soldiers in the South Drawing Room of the Royal Pavilion during its use as a Military Hospital, c.1915. Royal Pavilion & Museums.

SURVIVORS

Behind the Front

Canadian billets..............................

We had Canadian troops in Brighton from the beginning of 1942. I did a paper round (thin newspapers then, only four pages), and I would call on Canadian billets with leftover papers, and be invited into their cook-house at St. John's Church hall in Knoyle Road for flapjacks and maple syrup, a new treat for me. I helped at their canteen and cinema shows and was paid in Sweet Caporal cigarettes. I attended their weapon training instruction, and at the age of thirteen could strip and reassemble a Bren gun blindfolded.

The Royal Canadian Regiment visiting the Royal Pavilion during World War Two, 1940. Royal Pavilion & Museums.

I joined the 'D' company and cadets at Patcham, and was attached to the Home Guard Company at Preston Road/Carden Avenue.
.............**DAVID PAVEY**, *BRIGHTON BEHIND THE FRONT*

Sort of comments

The Canadians were very attractive to the girls, and attracted to the girls; this was because they generally had things which the local population did not have. They had cigarettes, sweets and confectionery of various kinds, they had chewing gum, which was considered a desirable commodity. As a boy, like many others of my age, I used to follow them round and say, "Have you got any gum, chum," the standard phrase used. They would generally give you some, and also quite often bars of chocolate, which were quite unobtainable. The Canadians, of course, had other ways of doing things, and other ways of talking, so a lot of the expressions were taken up by the girls especially, who liked aping the sort of comments that they made. They were extremely keen on ice hockey, almost their national sport, and this had a spin off on to the local team of Brighton Tigers, famous then, and for a long time after the war, at the SS Brighton, the sports stadium, at the bottom of West Street.
..........**BRIAN DUNGATE**, *BRIGHTON BEHIND THE FRONT*

Out of the water

My dad caught a mine cable one day in the War. There was a mine cable across Shoreham Harbour. 'Cos my dad was fishing in the War. He was exempt from the Army because it was essential work. They had to come in and put it on their net, and the chap who was with him said, "Look Bill," he said, "look what we got here then," he says, "it's a mine cable." He said, "What are we going to do?" So me dad says, "Well, there's only one thing to do," and he lifted it up and threw it back in!

SURVIVORS

Caught a lot of Germans, pulled a lot of Germans out of the water. The bombers used to crash, get shot down in the Channel. They had to tow them in. Dead pilots, and things like that.

He did a lot of work for Dr Parker [Brighton Medical Officer of Health]. He used to go testing the water and things. To see if it was safe. And he did all the fishing for the Aquarium, he was the only one who was allowed to catch fish to stock the Aquarium.
.... **DORIS WATHERINGTON**, *CATCHING STORIES*

Minesweepers

I got called up, joined up on my eighteenth birthday and went on minesweepers. Most of all these lads, all these fishermen, they all went on minesweepers. Well, they wanted fishermen, experienced seamen and that, you know, from all round the country, mostly longshore fishermen. I joined up ... and within eleven days I was on the boats. Well, all we done was a bit of rifle drill 'cos they knew we knew everything: we could tie ropes, splice, steer a boat, and that's all they wanted then, 1941 when I went up, but a lot of them went up the end of 1939.
.... **BOBBY ANDREW**, *CATCHING STORIES*

The Marie Leach

That's something I don't really much talk about. I belong to the Dunkirk Veterans' Association. I've got a certificate up there for the boat, that copper disc is what was issued for the boats, and that one's the British Expeditionary Force on it, and the certificate under it is signed by the Mayor of Dunkirk. That's my Dunkirk medal.

The Marie Leach. The Marie J Leach actually. But it was a horrible experience and something I'd like to cut out of my

> 'That's something I don't really much talk about'

mind. Getting the boats together and going down to Dover, and formulating at Folkestone and Dover for the crossing to proceed, that was quite exciting, I suppose, because many people there you met you knew. The adrenalin was flowing very freely. But when we started to go over there it was another story... horrible, horrible, absolutely horrible. Yes. Poor buggers, you saw them drop before you. Hundreds, thousands in fact.

And then of course after that, although I didn't go, a week after that they sent boats over to try to get them off of the coast at St. Valery. You never hear much about this.

Some of my cousins went over there, particularly one called Joseph Leach, he died since of course a few years ago, and he went over with a boat called, was it *The Breadwinner*? No I don't think it was *The Breadwinner*. Still, he went over there with a boat, and they went to St. Valery, but St. Valery's very much like Dover. Very high cliffs at St. Valery, where at Dunkirk there was sand and beaches. The troops were on the top of the cliff and they couldn't get them down, couldn't get them down to the boats. But you don't hear very much of St. Valery.

..... **JOHN LEACH**, *CATCHING STORIES*

Beall & Co. Cork merchant in Gardner Street, 1983 by Peter Chrisp.

SURVIVORS

The Doris

I know *The Doris* when she came back was full of bullet holes. The chap that's just died, Gillman, he repaired the holes, and he repaired them with corks, which he got in the Cork Shop in Gardner Street. My brother Bill made six trips to Dunkirk itself.
.... **JOE MITCHELL**, *CATCHING STORIES*.

The Dunkirk

Rachel: I shall never forget the time, Harry Marchant what was along of Ted, he was there and his Jim [Harry's brother], in his Sportsman, so he turned round and said to him, "Cor blimey, look at the herring," you know, Harry Marchant, and when the whatsername dropped down, the bomb, you talking about herring come up! Jimmy Howell's father was with us, he went, "Yeah." When I come home, I come home on the side of my feet like that, didn't I, when I come back from Dunkirk?

Elsie: Oh yeah, he had all them blisters.

Rachel: Where the paraffin had shot over the boat I took my boots off of course, something clever, I was going to swim back. Well, I didn't know no different. And the blisters I had, blisters like that, cor. I was in a rum state. Well, we had paraffin engines then, see. And when we got knocked about a bit, you see, there was cans of that had upset, and I took my boots off because I thought it might be a swimming job, of course the paraffin had got under the bottom of my feet, blisters. Oh, what a state, them. Yeah. Oh, they'll be nearly all dead, all that mob.

Elsie: There's not one of them left now, is there.

Rachel: Yeah. Well that's all I'm afraid I can tell you. When we got across there it was all over. My young brother, he was in the

Saladin, and they was bombing the shore till we got there. But when we got half-way across there was a French boat, small French boat, they was fetching some of them back, three dead in the boat. And they detailed one of these boats to take 'em back to Newhaven.

We volunteered. We needn't have gone. No, it was one of those things. There was a war on, you had your army over there. When they was chucking the bombs down we had colanders what you put on your head. Yeah, nothing. Bit of wood, hold a bit of wood up, stop a bullet. My boat got knocked to pieces, and I think they give us three pound ten. And as a skipper I got three pound ten, but I had to go to Eastbourne to pick it up. That was the *Marie Joyce*. Yes it was a hush-up job, that was. I've got a medal, yeah. To tell you the truth, I've never opened my medals from the War and I've never opened them for the Dunkirk, I gave them all to my grandchildren.

.... **RACHEL & ELSIE LEACH**, *CATCHING STORIES*

CHAPTER 3

Life After Stroke

Margaret Ward, front right, *Life After Stroke*, QueenSpark Books.

Life with Stroke

I came back............................

I suffered a stroke in the springtime of three years running. The first one was in the spring of 1988. I was at my son's house and they were handing round cups of tea in the middle of the afternoon, with biscuits, and I went to put my hand out to take a biscuit from a plate, and it dropped on the plate and I slumped over the settee, and I heard my daughter-in-law's mother say, "Oh, she's had a stroke." And I came back and I was all right. I don't know how long I was out for, but they just said, "Promise us you'll go to the doctor tomorrow." And I did that and he sent me to the neurologist to have a scan and I didn't feel any ill effects at all, nothing. But the neurologist said to me, "I'm sorry to tell you that you've had a slight stroke." So I said, "How do *you* know?" So he said to the nurse, "We've got a right one here, wait a minute, I'll show you." So he got the picture they had from the scan, and he said, "There's your head, look, there's your brain, and you see that big black bit there? Well that's dead and it'll never come back." And it never affected me in the least.
.............................**MARGARET**, *LIFE AFTER STROKE*

Months crawled by........................

My big stroke happened a year later. My ex-husband had decided to come home for three months from New Zealand after twenty-nine years away and I had offered to have him to stay for part of that time. We were going to make up for the lost years and try to find some happiness together once more. I was getting very excited as the months crawled by and his letters told me he was feeling the same.

LIFE AFTER STROKE

Two days before Jack was due to come I was taken ill. It was such a lovely evening and the bedding plants had arrived that morning so being the keen gardener I am and the ground all prepared, I went into the garden and started. There were three boxes of antirrhinums among many other boxes of plants, fifty in each box. I put in one hundred antirrhinums each side of the garden path. Normally I would have carried on and planted some more but I came over very tired as it was so hot. I had not bothered with dinner but still was not hungry so just had some biscuits and cheese. By this time it was bedtime so off I went and fell asleep very quickly.

In the morning I woke to find I could not move in bed, the whole of my left side was as useless as a log. The paralysis was completely down the left side. I lay there for a while very frightened. I knew it was a stroke and as I was in the house alone had to get help somehow. My phone was downstairs and from that day to this I shall never know how I reached it. I couldn't remember any phone numbers and didn't think of looking for them.

Quite suddenly my daughter's number came to me but when I tried to dial found my glasses were upstairs. I dialled the number by guesswork and this was hit and miss. Eventually my daughter answered and then to my amazement my speech would not come properly but I made her understand and she phoned her brother as he was nearer, in Woodingdean. He duly arrived and called the doctor, and my daughter and son-in-law came. When the doctor arrived he confirmed I had suffered a stroke. My first fear was that I might have another because of the slight one I'd had the year before.

When I had the big stroke my friend George who lives here was on holiday in London with his sister. So I was all alone. But he came back and he's been looking after me ever since.
.... **MARGARET**, *LIFE AFTER STROKE*

> '**My phone was downstairs and from that day to this I shall never know how I reached it**'

Cotton wool..................................

My third stroke came in the spring of 1990. I had been having bad headaches for about two weeks, in fact my head felt like cotton wool. I could not get going this special morning, having fully intended to dust my bedroom, but ended up cleaning the collection of teaspoons as it was a sitting down job. A few were ready and I was on my feet hanging them in their rack when my head started to spin and my right arm and leg went completely useless and I ended up hanging over the arm of the settee. I tried to say 'stroke' but the word would not come. In about two minutes I was back to normal, but not before being very scared. My friend called the doctor and he remembered I had experienced the same thing about two years previously so went back to the surgery to consult my notes. The brain scan I had had then showed that part of my brain had died but that had no lasting effect so I hoped this one would prove to be the same although I felt extremely tired and everything was an effort, also I still feel very giddy at times.
..........................MARGARET, *LIFE AFTER STROKE*

Recovery

Apathy..................................

Just after the stroke occurred, a state of apathy then took over; to sit in a chair and doze and be waited on was heaven. My mouth dropped to one side and I dribbled especially when drinking and had to use a kitchen towel for a bib. The district nurse came in for two days and washed me and did all the necessary ablutions including a suppository and then a physiotherapist came weekly and a stroke nurse every day giving me exercises to do to help my hand, arm, leg and feet. It was an effort to move any of these limbs.

My vision was impaired and I could only use my right hand. The whole body felt very heavy. New spectacles helped the vision, exercises helped the left side of my body and also with the apathy.
..........................**MARGARET,** *LIFE AFTER STROKE*

Right foot forward
One day she came in with a zimmer to aid me to try and walk. With this I could put the right foot forward and bring the left foot up to it by shuffling.

She spent a lot of time trying to put the left foot forward whilst I was leaning on the zimmer all the time. One day I was sitting in the lounge when I thought, "I will walk to that door without aid even if I fall over." Anyway I made it and called to my friend who had looked after me so well, "Look at me." My friend, who was in the garden, looked inside and was afraid to move in case I fell but gradually got me to a chair. I said, "Get rid of that zimmer, I will never use that again." It was slow work but I progressed from room to room and hanging on to the bannister rail with both hands went one stair at a time upstairs. My speech was coming back slowly, the power would not come behind the voice but they could hear me, swallowing was difficult but the nurse told me to stroke my throat.

The idea was to have an aim each week and to try to accomplish this was not easy. They gave me a very large clothes peg, which I had to squeeze with my left hand until I got it onto the edge of a paper, then came the smaller clothes pegs and then hair clips. In between doing this I had to turn the pages of a newspaper, this was very tedious and difficult but I managed it in the weeks allotted me.

The left arm would not stay down. When trying to walk, up it came to my chest with the fist clenched. So that was another aim,

> '**I will walk to that door without aid even if I fall over**'

to straighten the arm, and also the left knee was obstinate and was always bent, the exercise for these was to put one foot on a high stool and my hand flat on the table and keep bending and really straighten the knee. This was very difficult to do but the aim was accomplished.

Getting out of bed was another aim. They used to lay me flat on the bed, I had to turn over completely sideways, bend up the knees and get up on the bended elbow then swing the legs round. It is surprising how easy it becomes.

............................**MARGARET,** *LIFE AFTER STROKE*

> *'I am hoping this description will give everyone who has suffered a stroke the will to persevere'*

Confidence ....

After a few weeks the nurses started coming every other day until it got to twice a week, by this time I was walking with help down the garden path and back.

One day the nurse suggested she should take me in her car to the bus terminus at the White Horse in Rottingdean and ask the driver if I could practise getting on and off the stationary bus to give me confidence. I did this three times, sitting in the bus each time, and the driver was most co-operative. From then on we hired a taxi to take us into the village once a week and went into the Queen Victoria for a drink and came back on the bus. It was so lovely to get out and meet some of my friends again after all these months. Of course my close friends had been visiting quite often once the nurse allowed it.

One or two falls occurred while trying to make progress. Once I went flat on my face in the kitchen tripping over the metal strip in the outer door, and then I tried to reach a wall cupboard by standing on a stool, overbalanced flat on my back and cracked the back of my head. The third time I fell in the Queen Victoria loo, banging my head on the floor quarry tiles, getting up with one hand on the paper holder and the other on the door handle. Of course there was no strength in the left hand and I was very frightened. I swear I will never again lock a loo door as it was a painful effort to get up and no-one could get in. I think I damaged a rib as it took weeks to get better and also undermined my confidence, but this soon came back after a few weeks.

I am hoping this description will give everyone who has suffered a stroke the will to persevere until they get back the full use of their limbs.

............................**MARGARET**, *LIFE AFTER STROKE*

CHAPTER 4

Working Folk

Fishermen on Brighton beach by a capstan, c.1860. Royal Pavilion & Museums.

Long Hours

Celluloid cuffs ....

I was aware of someone shaking me and saying, "Get up." I could not open my eyes because of a bright light. It was my sister's voice and the electric light was new to me. At home was a gas light downstairs, and candles in the bedrooms. "Hurry up," she said. "It's half past five. I'll leave my bedroom door open, you come along to me when you are dressed."

I felt dazed and very tired. I had hardly slept all night. The mattress was so different from the 'shake-up' beds at home and the pillow was hard. But I got out of bed, pulled the tin trunk from under it, and dressed myself in my maid's apron, celluloid cuffs and collar, and lastly the 'Dorcas' cap. The last item took longest as I had to do my hair up in a bun, or somehow put all strands out of sight.

As my hair was only a 'long bob' I used two packets of hairpins and even they were not successful as during the day they dropped out, sometimes down my

Ovingdean Hall, c.1913. James Gray Collection.

WORKING FOLK

neck or tinkling on the floor, so adjustments had to be made with the pins not lost.

I went to my sister's room, carefully switching off my light and together we walked along the uncarpeted corridor, down the bare twisting stairs, along another passage, across a concrete yard, through a squeaky swing door, and we were in the school quarters. My sister could now leave go my hand as we were in the light again.

Ovingdean Hall had its own electric light generator, but we had to go very carefully or it faded out. We maids were always accused of wasting it if ever there was a failure, although we were conscious of the problem. But who knew that after 'lights out' we were reading our paperbacks in bed? Only when a voice from outside shouted, "Put that light out," we'd switch off till the footsteps retreated and switch on again.

My sister and I went to the housemaid's cupboard, loaded ourselves with broom, brush, dustpan, duster, polishers and a 'swinger'. This was a heavy contraption for polishing floors. Too heavy to lift, it was dragged. It consisted of thick bristles in a block of wood about 10 by 14 inches, on this was a layer of lead for the weight, another piece of wood on top of that, then a long handle was fixed to a bar so that it could be swung from side to side, following the lay of the floorboards. There was an art in using this which did not need so much energy but for a while I felt my whole frame was being torn apart.

The polish for the floors was beeswax and turpentine, which we put in large stone marmalade jars. We asked the cook's permission to stand them on the large kitchen range when no food was about. The kitchen was her holy of holies and all knocked on the door and waited till told to enter, but mostly she answered one at the door.

> **'I felt my whole frame was being torn apart'**

My duties as third dormitory maid were before breakfast, clean and polish two classrooms, one flight of stairs to be scrubbed, go up to the dormitories to fill washing basins with hot water for the seventeen boys in my dormitories. It was carried from the bathroom in two and a half gallon cans, one in each hand, along a long corridor, as mine were at the other end. Weren't those cans heavy! They were as much as I wanted to carry, then stand one down while I lifted the other to pour water in the bowls. Three or four journeys were required before all had water. There was no early morning cup of tea. Breakfast was at 7.30 a.m., and we took our seats in our station of staff... There was half an hour for breakfast, then upstairs to make beds and empty the slops in the dormitories. I had seventeen beds to make, pyjamas to fold, dressing gowns to hang up and wash basins to attend to, chambers to empty and lock away. Every boy had his own square wash-stand, a basin and jug let into a hole on top, under his shelf on which was tooth mug, soap dish, a dish for toothbrush and flannel and a small medicine glass. In a cupboard underneath was the chamber pot.

Armed with two slop-pails and cloths we daily went about the emptying, rinsing and cleaning of each one. It was a bit of a rush for the pails as there were only four and if the other two maids got them I would have to start making beds. Then I seemed to find the toilets occupied when I wanted to empty mine, but in time I was as artful as them, I'd hide a couple when I took up the early morning washing water.

All morning work had to be completed and everyone washed and changed into their afternoon black by midday when it was our lunchtime. Then we went into the school dining room to wait at tables on the boys. I had two tables and it was journeys from the kitchen hatch, backwards and forwards, fetching and carrying for an hour. Then all set for washing up silver and glasses in our

WORKING FOLK

pantry. All dishes and large plates went back to the kitchen to be washed in large wooden sinks. In the afternoon we had jobs according to the day.

Mondays was all Sunday suits to be brushed and marks sponged off before putting away. On other days there was sock sorting and darning, linen mending, silver polishing, etc. We always had something to help keep us out of mischief.

Tea was a more leisurely meal for us and the boys, but at ten minutes to seven each evening we had to go to chapel. Then the headmaster's wife would be behind us to make sure we were all there. She had a way of knowing what staff were on or off duty and if one were missing she had an uncanny sense of knowing where they were, and almost dragging them in. This is how life went on daily, but as I got used to the atmosphere of the place, I felt more confidence in myself, and more happy than at first. The girls were alright when I got to know them and we had fun at times.

.... **DAISY NOAKES,** *THE TOWN BEEHIVE*

'I felt more confidence in myself, and more happy than at first'

Daisy Noakes,
The Town Beehive,
QueenSpark Books.

One shilling a day

Mother... at 12 she left school to look after her nine brothers and sisters, while her mother went to a hand laundry and did ironing from 7 a.m. to 7 p.m. for one shilling a day in 1880. Father left home at 12 – his father did a lot of betting – used to have rows in the house. He left home, walked to Newhaven and took a job on the docks. He went to Lewes and worked in a grocery shop for quite a while. I think that's where he got the idea of having the shop. His brother had a shop at the top of the hill – we used to come there – we liked the look of it – it was through Dad seeing how well he got on that made him do it. He could get a job from here perhaps and they could live here and perhaps the shop would be enough to carry on. They worked hard, very hard.

MISS BRISTOW, *SHOPS BOOK*

> '50 sovereigns in those days was a terrific lot'

What hours were you open?

They paid £50 for the incoming of the shop – goodwill and stock and everything. When we started selling and people came and asked for stuff, it was all dummies – two dozen bottles of Sarson's Vinegar – all doubles, the whole lot. It was all fake. He couldn't do anything and 50 sovereigns in those days was a terrific lot. Whole lot of their money had gone. Dad explained to one or two wholesalers how he had been let down and they let him have stuff on sale or return – gradually he built the business up. After a few months he'd got it on its feet, you know. He bought a little Russian pony and trolley and he went all round the streets selling stuff. Mother carried on at the shop and looked after my brother and I and did all the cooking and made all the clothes.

Dad got up at 4:00 or 5:00 in the morning – until midnight we were open. Every day, and Christmas Day was the day you

WORKING FOLK

took most money. They had the money, you see. Father said he had to keep open because he wanted the money. He began to get on his feet.

MISS BRISTOW, *SHOPS BOOK*

4:00 in the morning

Mrs Wheatley remembers her father doing a round with a barrow: "He gave up his barrow work just after mother had the shop. He used to leave the house at about 8:00 – at one time he had a donkey and trolley. He went all up Ditchling Road way – he knocked on doors and he had some regular customers up there. Mother got up at 4:00 in the morning – down the Market, buy her stuff – come back, have an hour's rest – cup of tea and go back down to see it delivered – to see it was put on the van or you might lose it. Mother was a very good businesswoman.

"I'll tell you how badly off we were then – we hadn't got a chair to sit on – we were sitting on boxes, and mother had to wash my brother's shirt Friday to be clean Monday for school."

MRS WHEATLEY, *SHOPS BOOK*

We charged 2d.

Some people used to make their own bread and we used to bake it – a farthing a loaf. On Friday afternoons they all used to bring their cakes and we used to bake them for them. One penny for that. Sundays, they'd bring their Sunday dinners; we charged 2d. Christmas dinners, we charged 8d. for a leg of pork and chicken, 1s. for turkeys – that's basted and everything. He used to have one man to help him like – in the bakehouse. He'd push the bread round on a barrow.

You had to buy the flour off the miller in them days. See,

the miller owned all the bakeries. He rented it and paid £150 goodwill when he went in. The miller was Smith of Britannia Mill, Portslade. They'd deliver flour each week and collect rent every quarter. It was tied, see.

In them days you had to work long hours. I used to start in the bakery with him about half past five, and we worked till 11.00am. Then we pushed the barrow round till about 5.00 in the afternoon – downtown and up Elm Grove. We came back to sweep the bakehouse up and chop wood and get the coal in. I used to get 5s. a week. I finished at 7.30pm; he said I wouldn't wear out, but I'd perhaps rust out.

.... MR HIDER, *SHOPS BOOK*

Lower, the Baker in Brighton Place (or the Knab). Drawing by William Thomas Quartermain. Royal Pavilion & Museums.

Deliveries ....

We all, and the men, used to do other deliveries in the afternoon, see – they'd do furniture moving on the vans. We also did brick carting, sand carting. In the mornings they was all out hawking. Used to start 4.00am at the station weighing up and loading up five horses and carts before 8:00. 8:15 bell would go at the works – home and have breakfast, then we went out. Father went out hawking just the same. Me and mother used to go round collecting money and mother helped with the books... it was a profitable business.

Men had to look after the horses – had to come in of a morning and

WORKING FOLK

water them. Sometimes Dad used to go down about 6:00 and water them and feed them. Often there wasn't much work in the afternoon – they never knocked off – there was always something to do – painting the vans up, washing them down, cleaning the harness. They'd finish about 5:00 or 6:00. I left school at 14 and worked up to 8:00 at night.

.................................MR GRINYER, *SHOPS BOOK*

The day's bread............................

As Mr Grinyer's comments suggest, the working shopkeeper kept long hours. Before the shop even opened in the morning, the greengrocer had to buy and transport his produce from the market, which opened at 4.00am. At 5:30, the baker had to start making the day's bread; the coal merchant had to weigh and load up at the station at 4.00am. The shops then opened at 8:00 and closed when people stopped coming – usually at 8:30 in the evening on a weekday, but frequently as late as midnight on Saturdays. The keen competition amongst working shopkeepers and with professionals, as well as the working hours of their customers, meant that opening hours had to be long.
.......*SHOPS BOOK*

S. F. Deveson & Son Greengrocers, 58 Lewes Road, c.1930s. Royal Pavilion & Museums.

Picket Duty

> 'They came out on their horses with whacking long sticks, and they were smashing people down in the streets'

The miners

In 1919 the miners went on strike and we gave them our support. I was made a member of the union in January, as an apprentice. The secretary, doing his normal job, didn't ask whether you wanted to do picket duty. He simply went down the list of names and numbers and put you on picket duty. So I found myself at the age of fourteen at five o'clock in the morning on picket duty outside the works at Brighton, with policemen all round the gate and everything.

In 1921 we were on strike again over the travelling time of the men who had to go from Brighton to Lancing to work. They were claiming that they should be paid for travelling in the train. I was working in Brighton then, and we went on strike to support them over it. It came to nothing though of course. The management had the free transport arguments on their side.

But 1926 was different. That was a ruthless strike, absolutely ruthless. The strange part about it, what wasn't realised, was the strength of the trade union movement. It was so strong that it overwhelmed us. Everybody was coming out, our foreman, everybody in authority came out with us, so long as they were on a wage basis. We stopped everything, we were so powerful. And yet we weren't prepared to govern with it. We couldn't, because we didn't have the organisational ability to manoeuvre all that great power. There was terrific enthusiasm for it. It was remorseless. It was so remorseless that it got serious. There was civil strife everywhere. Even in Brighton, which at one time had a hundred thousand majority for a Conservative, we were up in arms attacking blackleg transport, and the police. They

WORKING FOLK

came out on their horses with whacking long sticks, and they were smashing people down in the streets, I went to a meeting and the policeman walked all along the road at the side kicking my feet, trying to make me fall down, so that I should only just clutch hold of him. Then I could be had for obstructing the police. But I never did clutch hold of him, I went home, and I was frightened to death, because I wasn't doing anything wrong, I was just going to an ordinary meeting.

I was working with the man who was a shareholder. He was against the General Strike. So when they called us out on strike, I stayed on working with him. I was still quite young. I carried on working there for an hour or two. Then a message was sent in by somebody in the works, "If you don't come out on strike with your mates, we'll put you in the horse-trough." They used to have troughs filled with water in the streets for the horses. There was one outside the works. It didn't take me long to get out after that.

Then Sir John Simon gave the word that the General Strike was against the law, and everybody suddenly became frightened and wanted to go back to work. It was the most amazing transformation I've ever known in my life. It was only because he gave the official announcement, as a law man, that it was against the law, that everybody thought, "Oh crumbs, what's going to happen? We're going to lose our jobs." So it was back to work. But the movement should never have collapsed under it. We had the power then, and we should have gone on, but it was too much for us. The power was too big. We couldn't grasp it – it was like going to the moon.
.... JOHN LANGLEY, *ALWAYS A LAYMAN*

> 'The power was too big. We couldn't grasp it – it was like going to the moon'

On the Buses

Spotless
The small amount of time I've been on the buses has seen many changes. You often hear them bemoaning the fact they used to have their own buses. My first full-time mate used to come in in the morning about 1½ hours before he was supposed to and polish the bus, shine all the lamps up, wipe the seats. It was a pleasure to drive a bus after him because it was so spotless. Actually it makes you feel old when your first bus brake handle was made of brass.

BRIGHTON ON THE ROCKS

Double Decker bus 1A in Portslade, 1969. Royal Pavilion & Museums.

Rather OK
I came into the bus industry at the rough end when it was suffering greatly, first from the transformation from a private industry, which was on the wane, and unfortunately a lot of our branch members look back to those days with a certain pride because the bus company was making money.

Also the boom of the late 60s and 70s was still in operation and nobody wanted to work in our job because the pay was so poor. Before the war a

WORKING FOLK

bus driver was regarded as something rather OK (two suits in the wardrobe and a holiday abroad or away). When I joined, it was the last resort or the crazy desire to drive a great vehicle... When I started we had 18 1s and 2s running out of Whitehawk Garage. We've now got something like four. The garage was crammed full. I used to look forward to work because it was different. Even today there's no way you can call it boring. It can be frustrating, soul-destroying, but never boring. There was a certain friendliness then because you were on the same routes all the time. You get to know the people and their quirks. Some talk to you and some are rude to you, and you gradually get to know how to deal with them all... It becomes a part of your life. I think the public also regret that they don't have the same drivers... and of course they had a conductor with them too who was their mate.
.... *BRIGHTON ON THE ROCKS*

> **'You get to know the people and their quirks'**

Thing of the past ....
Now conductors are a thing of the past. Our governor gave the last seven conductors at our depot (Whitehawk) the sack last year. It's much to our discredit... our members have sold out our workmates. We hung on in our depot for a long time. We did succumb under the usual economic threats of redundancies and, "If we don't make cuts... then it's the best thing, chaps."

It's almost countrywide now, OPO (one-person-operated). It takes a certain type of person to be able to cope with OPO. You have to be determined to treat the job as two separate jobs (for ¼ more wages). I've seen men go one-manning who have always been cheerful... and within three or four months they drive past you and they've got a perpetual frown on their face and they blow up at the slightest thing... If you watch a busman on holiday, it usually takes him three days to stop looking at his watch... When you're OPO you've got this psychological pressure from management to keep those schedules running (you used to get fined for running late). Then there's a pressure, particularly near a meal break or finishing time. There's the pressure, perhaps you'll not believe this, of worry that the passengers are late for work, psychological pressure from the queue.

It's difficult to say how OPO has affected the times of schedules. From the 50s you had an extra minute from Hove Town Hall to the Old Steine. You're still supposed to run to the same time. You get 10 minutes to do it; 19 minutes from Portslade Station to the Old Steine; 35 minutes from the Old Steine to Rottingdean. But you have quicker vehicles...

.... *BRIGHTON ON THE ROCKS*

Stress

There is still stress. The stress of potential accidents... there's always been a high heart disease among bus drivers, backache, stomachs. I'm told the life expectancy of a bus driver is lower than a miner.

Wages have deteriorated. I take home £96 after tax. If you take off 25% for OPO bonus and give me a conductor back and allow for inflation and increased tax, I'm probably about the same as when I started. That's for 48 hours. On 40 hours I would take home about £75 maximum.

We have been continuously forced over the years by management, and by the national union negotiators, to work overtime in order to earn a normal decent living... At last year's wage negotiation we went up to double time for Saturday working. For years and years we've been told we've got to work overtime. They've had long schedules and the only time they've brought them down is when the legal requirement makes

'You really don't know what shift work is like until you've worked it... You become a different person. Shift work is terrible for a family'

WORKING FOLK

them do it. You could see notices up on our boards every day requesting blokes to go and work overtime. We've got blokes who do seven days a week plus overtime every day. It's an eight-hour day now. The longest duty when I started was a 10½ hour shift and no meal break, and that's hard. The union have continually increased the shift rate and overtime rate, so they have encouraged it... You really don't know what shift work is like until you've worked it... You become a different person. Shift work is terrible for a family. There must be a bigger divorce rate on the buses than any job I've ever come across. This new system means there's no way a married man will ever see his children, nor watch a continuing series on TV, nor go to night school, on a regular basis. You're on your own.
.... *BRIGHTON ON THE ROCKS*

Someone Has To Do It

Graffiti...................................
I mean, it's a fact – it's just a job. Even if toilet cleaning is not everybody's idea of a job, it is an essential occupation. Someone has to do it, and it is not as bad as people think. It can be mucky when the public leave the toilet dirty. But, it has its funny side.

Graffiti – that was everywhere. We used to have lovely little messages left. I won't use the language, because it doesn't come in my vocabulary. I went over to the Steine and saw a red blob on the wall and – "What the devil's that?" It was a lovely poem, which went sideways down the wall, three verses long, and when I got round the corner I found a beautiful drawing. Very explicit! It took me two and a half hours to get it off. It was only lipstick. I think they must have used a whole tube. I wasn't very happy at the end of the day. I had to keep going backwards and forwards – "Oh, I've been over this. Have another go! Oh, have another go..."

BRIGHTON'S UNSUNG HEROES

Joan Parsons, *Jobs for Life*, QueenSpark Books.

In some cases you can get it off and in some cases you can't. If it's on tiles you can, to a certain degree, but it takes ages. We used to have cream for tiles, but you can't use that for the doors, but when they started using oil-based pens – you can't get it off. And then they started using spray paint. More often then not, it was a case of, "Leave it." You can't get it off. The more you try the more you rub off the original paint.

JOAN PARSONS, *JOBS FOR LIFE*

Paper everywhere...........................

Hidden cameras in loos would be very interesting. If you could stand it! I mean, really and truly, I'm not being funny, but it amazes me why people have to go into a loo and drop paper on the floor. I was helping out one Sunday at the Colonnade on the seafront. I had to wait for the actual attendant to come, and when we got inside we just looked and – "What the hell's happened?"

There was paper everywhere, even

Public lavatories in the Old Steine, which were closed and converted into a café in 1999. Royal Pavilion & Museums.

WORKING FOLK

hanging from the light fittings. Somebody had been in there before they'd locked up the previous night and emptied every holder. It was just like paper decorations. They were loose leaves, from the little packs. When we saw it we just stood and looked at each other. I think they must have wet them and they'd stuck to the light bulbs. I don't think they'd missed anywhere.

The Corporation paid a lot of money to re-do the Gents by the Bandstand. The following week someone set fire to it. All the wiring was burnt and congealed. They couldn't afford to strip it out again. So, they had to close it.

............................**JOAN PARSONS,** *JOBS FOR LIFE*

Waiting for the ladies at the Aquarium, 1977 by David Fisher.

The Gardens

Male, female, they used to sleep in the Gardens. They'd come down and I'd be sweeping up and they'd just look at me and say, "What are you doing?" They didn't know what time of day it was. They used to come in and sit in the toilets and drink their cans and bottles and they either left them on the floor or put them in the bins. Some of them were very nice. Like everybody else who had a drink, some would just laugh, but others would get jumpy. I think half the time those that do turn nasty haven't got the money to buy any more to top themselves up. It's no good shouting at them, because if they're that far gone they just don't know what you're saying. It's no good telling a man who's three parts to the wind to sober up. He just looks at you as if to say, "What's she talking about? – and, yes, I'll have another bottle."

At night, if they could get in when no one was around, they'd sleep there. There were one or two who did that at the Clock Tower. At Rock Gardens there was one lady, that was her home. She more or less moved in. But, she died, poor soul. I only saw her once or twice. She used to keep herself in the one loo, and if you hadn't got the key with you, you couldn't open it. She slept in there; she had everything in there; all her goods and chattels.

Two or three used to sleep at Norfolk Square, and you had to get them out to clean. Some of them got quite nasty if you woke them up. I used to say, "If you don't move you'll have to sleep in the dirt." Some would move because they wanted the place cleaned up, but others used to get quite nasty about being moved on. I would say, "Well, I'm not chucking you out. You can come back when I've finished."

We had one, she used to have a great big shopping trolley with all her goods in and, oh, she used to get very annoyed. At times,

> 'Some would move because they wanted the place cleaned up, but others used to get quite nasty about being moved on'

she was very, very aggressive. I was cleaning the floor, and went to push the door open, and she told me to so-and-so off. I swept the stairs down and came back and she was still there, so I said, "Well just let me clean up in there..." and Oh! She came out with a mouthful of vile words. I went and got some water and when I came back she had gone. But, when I went to wash the steps, her trolley was still up there. And she swore black was white that I'd pinched her stuff out of her trolley – her fur coat and everything.

JOAN PARSONS, *JOBS FOR LIFE*

An easy job.............................

It's an easy job, but... I wasn't enamoured of going to Norfolk Square because they have a seat between the toilets, you know, and all the winos sit there, men and women, and sometimes you had really nasty things said to you. And some things are hard to ignore – especially when you get insulted right, left and centre and you can't answer back. That always gave me the willies. I used to go there and think, "I wonder if I can get in and out before they come round."

JOAN PARSONS, *JOBS FOR LIFE*

On the Sea

Fishing

My first grown-up way of fishing was when I was helping on the boats down at the fish market, which was situated on the Lower Esplanade, and I used to go down there and I used to go out on the ferry boats and the big trawlers used to land their fish on the ferry boats and we used to bring the fish from the big trawlers on the beach. And we used to carry the big boxes of fish up by hand.

Fish market on lower esplanade, c.1960. Royal Pavilion & Museums.

And in those days a box used to take ten or twelve stone of fish in each box, and it used to take two of us, two of the lads from the school, to help get them up the beach. Then we used to grade the fish on the fish market. This was early in the morning by the way, at six or seven o'clock in the morning before you went to school. For this work, helping them get the fish to the fish market, up the beach, we used to receive five or six little fish each. Just enough for one of us to eat! Then as we gradually got older and we got more sensible, we were able to mate up with the fishing trawlers, and we used to go out ourselves and help catch them, and shooting the nets and pulling the nets in.

LEN TRUSSELL, *CATCHING STORIES*

WORKING FOLK

Lost at sea..........

All our relatives were at sea, yes. My Uncle Jim. I had a great-uncle that was lost at sea, on a very calm night, as the ship was coming about the boom caught him and knocked him overboard. In those days the fishermen wore very heavy leather boots to keep them on deck in any rough weather. Not like the rubber ones of today. And therefore he never stood a chance of swimming.

.... **JIM SINDEN**, *CATCHING STORIES*

Fishing with fathers ....

We picked up our knowledge from the fishermen, and that's how we got the information.

As we grew older, and we mixed with fishermen, we still had the knowledge gradually going into our head – let's say, well, the knowledge gradually grew on you. Whoever you went fishing with, a lot of people, they went fishing with their fathers, and that's how it went on. Picking all this knowledge up. That's who they were getting it from. Who else could you get it from? It all starts from knowledge, as you probably know.

............................**DICK TAYLOR**, *CATCHING STORIES*

Fishing boat nearly capsizing as she comes in to the beach, *Catching Stories*, QueenSpark Books.

'It all starts from knowledge, as you probably know'

Get the nets

Well, I can remember this, it was before I left school, we got caught again in the thunder and lightning storm, and as soon as it started thunder and lightning my old dad said, "Get to work – get the nets in quick!" Well, we got these nets in, and we were running for Shoreham Harbour. Well, at Shoreham there used to be a sandbar run out back of Shoreham and the seas used to break over it when the wind was southerly, and the tide coming out of Shoreham, and my old dad said to this fellow, "Get one of them drums of paraffin up on the side," and, "it used to have a cork in it, you know?" And my dad opened it up and said, "Hold your hand underneath it, tight, and when I say 'Let it go,' let it go." I can hear him now. So, the sea was going to break on us, and this paraffin went on the water and quietened it down. Before that, my dad said, "Take your boots off." Oh dear, when he said that I thought, "Right – we're going in for a swim here!"

JOHNNY HUMPHREY, *CATCHING STORIES*

Early hours

I used to think he's late, no he's stuck in the pub! I have sat indoors all night when they've been fishing, when they've come in early hours of the morning, but I always made sure there was a big fire and a big saucepan of soup on the stove, 'cos he used to bring half the fishing fleet home. But it was always there, and I never ever went to bed unless he was home as I repeat myself again, I've sat there all night sometimes when he's been out. You do get used to it really you know but the first time of doing it is very nerve-racking, you think, "My God, what the hell's happened here?" Now they've got these – I've just got rid of mine – ship-to-shore radios. We had one bought, we've had one for a long time, but there was nothing like that then.

BARBARA GILLAM, *CATCHING STORIES*

WORKING FOLK

Local boats..............................

One of our boats come in, one of our local boats, they came in because it was blowing hard. One of them, the *Our Boys*, belonged to old Buck Ennis, who was a local fisherman. His son was on there, Fred. And they come in the night. Fred stayed aboard, he wasn't going to go home, and he got worried in the night that Sammy Andrews and *Our Maggie* hadn't arrived back in harbour. So they sent the lifeboat out after him. And poor old Sam was out there broke down, so they towed him in. I'll never forget this. I was one of the launchers of the lifeboat, and as the lifeboat towed the old boat up the harbour, there was old Sammy there steering his old boat, because they had no wheelhouse, they had to stand out there and steer their boat – they never had wheelhouses, they didn't know what a wheelhouse was, they stood out and took everything – and as he come up the harbour there he was drinking a cup of tea, he had his old mug of tea in his hand, as though nothing had happened!
..........................**BOB HOLDEN**, *CATCHING STORIES*.

CHAPTER 5

Community

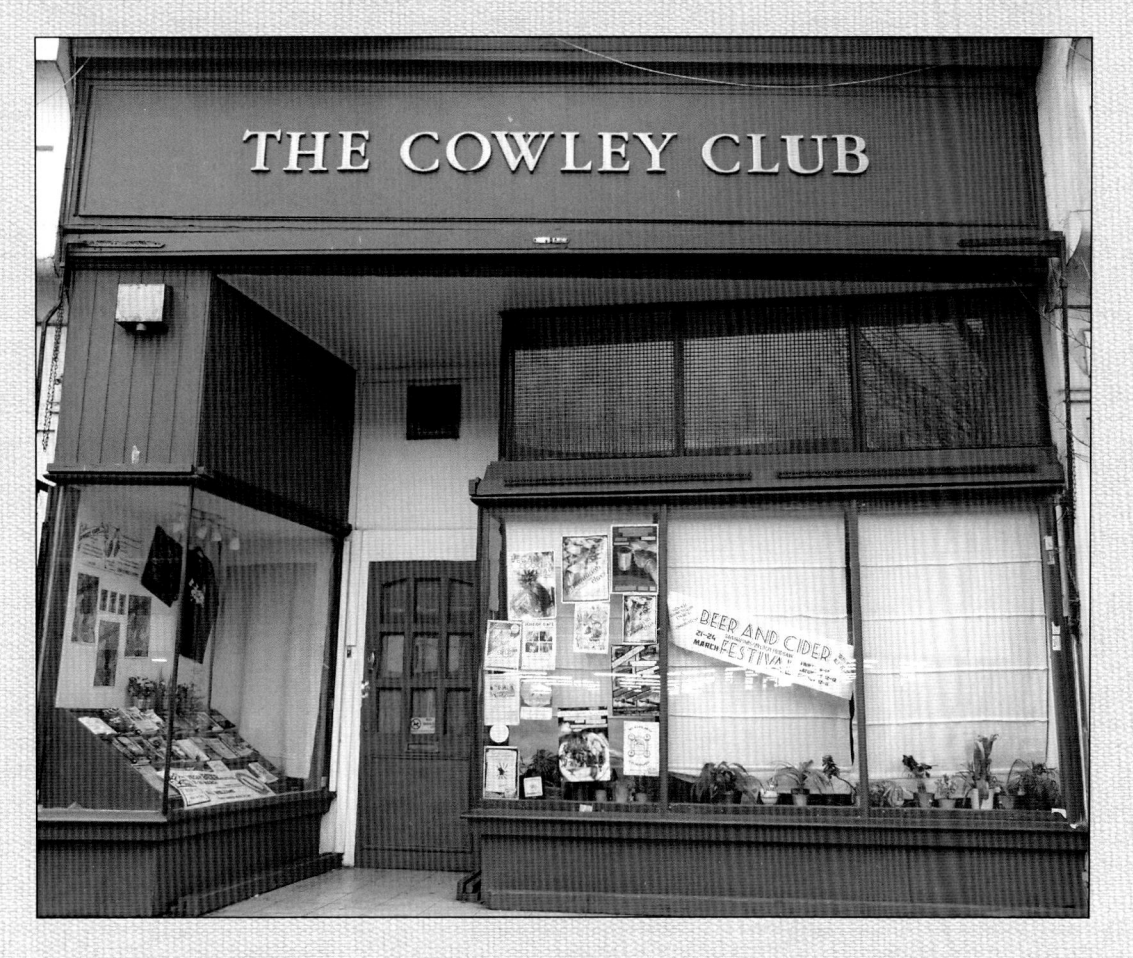

The Cowley Club, home of the Migrant English Project, 2019 by Ali Ghanimi.

BRIGHTON'S UNSUNG HEROES

Caring

'We would walk to Middle St. Synagogue as it was the only place of worship then'

Coffee and homemade cake.....................

As soon as I arrived at Yetta's home in Langdale Rd., Hove, I was offered coffee and homemade cake by this charming lady, who looked nearer 60 than her 80 years. Yetta, a 2nd generation Brit, was born in London in 1912, but came to Brighton in 1917 during the First World War. The family took over a sweet shop (where her brother was born) in Warleigh Rd., Brighton, near Preston Circus, and lived above it.

"We went to Preston Rd. School... now part of the Poly," she told me, "until I left at 14. We were the only Jewish children there, as few Jews lived in that area. But we were excused assembly and allowed time off for the Jewish Holidays. We would walk to Middle St. Synagogue as it was the only place of worship then. Most of the Jews lived around the North Laine and I remember going to the butcher and grocer in Bond St. and Gardner St. I believe the delicatessen in Gardner St. still exists, but I don't think it is Jewish any more."

After leaving school, she was apprenticed to hairdressing at

Middle Street Synagogue, 2012 by Jvhertum.

COMMUNITY

'Collins Salon' in the arcade off Western Rd., and trained there for two years. When she was 20, she met and married Nat Rose, who was a theatrical agent. Unfortunately he became ill with TB after only being married for a few weeks. He died three years later, leaving her with a young son of 18 months.

When her mother died in 1958, she realised that her true talents lay in 'caring'... whether for sick, disabled or handicapped, so she gave up hairdressing and joined the British Red Cross Society. After passing exams she became cadet officer, training girls of 6-14 at Red Cross Headquarters in Montpelier Crescent.

Not content with this, she offered her services as nursing help in the Children's Hospital and Brighton General, and finally, for 6 years she was Matron of the Spastic Centre in Dyke Rd. (now demolished).
.... *WE'RE NOT ALL ROTHSCHILDS!*

£28.00 a month..............................

She was now 50, and with all her experience she felt that she wanted to qualify as a professional nurse. But at her age it was difficult and daunting to start as a probationer with 18-year-olds. "However," she told me, "with the help of a lady doctor I knew, who encouraged me and as I had prior knowledge of physiology and anatomy from my work in the Red Cross, my doctor friend persuaded the matron of the New Sussex Hospital in Windlesham Rd. to take me on."

She went on, "I trained and worked at that hospital until it closed in 1982 to become a psychiatric hospital. I did two years' training as SEN for £28.00 a month plus uniform and laundry, but despite coming out top in the final exams, I decided against carrying on to SRN as I wanted to nurse – not to do admin work.

I became acting Staff Nurse and was in charge of wards until I retired at 63."
................................*WE'RE NOT ALL ROTHSCHILDS!*

Badge of honour

But that wasn't the end of her career. Yetta continued to do supply nursing and voluntary work for the Red Cross. Apart from first aid and welfare work, she counselled, ran disabled clubs, helped at Red Cross shops and did escort duties taking patients to and from hospital.

She now has a Badge of Honour medal as a life member of the Red Cross. She said, "I've had a hard life, but my retirement years have been the best ever. I've had some wonderful experiences and memories."
................................*WE'RE NOT ALL ROTHSCHILDS!*

> 'I've had a hard life, but my retirement years have been the best ever'

Windlesham House, New Sussex Hospital for Women, c.1920s. James Gray Collection.

COMMUNITY

Trans Brighton

Awesome ....
I work for Allsorts and I run Transformers, which is the group for young trans people, which myself and my colleague Elliot were asked if we wanted to start. It's the first project of its kind in the city. It's specifically designed for young transgender people and the work that we do with them is awesome.

We go to schools and do training for young people and staff and educational professionals. We worked with the Charlotte Miller art project to produce the *Being Human* photography book. We produced the *Trans Toolkit* with the Healthy Schools team, which is basically an instruction manual on how to support trans people.

I totally believe that a safe space is essential. Somewhere we can go and nurture one another and lick our wounds if we're hurt and encourage ourselves and support one another. Where you can go and just be like, "This is our space," and put our flag up and do stuff without anyone bothering us, that's essential.

This is a wonderful town. It's got its flaws and it's a hotbed of sleaze, isn't it? Which I quite like. It's a wonderful place to transition because it's small and there is an actual community here, of people who really love and respect each other. It is more open-minded on the whole, like I've walked past many a building site and not had any grief off of anyone. I mean that's really sort of stereotypical, but I've pigeon-holed people, expecting them to be a certain way and they haven't been. It's just a good town. I'm proud to call it my home.
.... **MAEVE**, *BRIGHTON TRANS*FORMED*

> '**It's a wonderful place to transition... there is an actual community here, of people who really love and respect each other**'

Refuge

Opportunity............................

The Migrant English Project (MEP) was started by about six of us who wanted to campaign on the politics of state borders and migration issues at a time when the government and the Home Office were cracking down on migrants. In addition to campaigning, we also wanted to help migrants in more direct practical terms. In both the UK and Europe there is a major problem with migrants becoming isolated. One of the biggest restrictions placed on migrants by the government is that of not being able to work. They are unable to gain experience and, even when they have refugee status, they don't have an understanding of how to deal with the job-seeking environment. We realized that, for a migrant, learning the language of the host country is the most important step towards finding their feet in a new environment. As the Cowley Club was closed on Mondays, it proved to be the ideal place to hold English classes.

For many of the teachers it was a fantastic opportunity to gain experience and, as always at the Cowley Club, there were people turning up at the door and offering to help in the café or with teaching or the cooking.

We produced a leaflet and had it translated into about ten languages. We distributed it to solicitors and local community organizations. We established relationships with the universities and colleges like BHASVIC and City College. We also had people referred to us from advice and mentoring projects for refugees and asylum seekers. Before long we had a huge network of friends and contacts.
....*REFUGE*

COMMUNITY

Respect

On an average Monday at the MEP there'll be about thirty students with ten or twelve volunteer tutors. There are as many people as there are chairs, and we're beginning to run out of space. Amongst the students there'll be anything up to a dozen nationalities.

It might be thought that there would be difficulties having to accommodate people that come from such a diverse range of cultural backgrounds, but it has never presented a problem. We have found that all that is needed is respect and consideration; beyond that, we have never had to be anything other than ourselves... We offer support, advice and information for people going through the Asylum process in a relaxed, safe and unthreatening environment. The teachers, in particular, build close and trusting relationships with individual students and are able to give them a great deal of personal encouragement.

REFUGE

The Migrant English Project

The origins of the MEP were political and it has always worked on asylum cases and anti-deportation campaigns. We have, on at least one occasion, been able to prevent the deportation of one our students.

The MEP's independence is possibly its greatest strength. And we are very careful to avoid doing anything that would compromise our freedom of action. We have no connections with the church or any government agencies and have, in the past, rejected funding because we felt it would place limitations and obligations on us. Our independence is vitally important, as it is one of the main reasons that the people who come here feel they can place absolute trust in us.

> 'We have found that all that is needed is respect and consideration'

What is amazing, is how naturally the MEP developed beyond being just a place for teaching English, how it became a social club, a place where people are brought together and a place where so much has been done to break down the isolation that is felt by many refugees and asylum seekers.
....*REFUGE*

Language ....

Language is a problem for us both. Learning is difficult. In Kenya we both learnt Swahili very fast just by listening and talking to the people we met. Here it's hard to practise. English people don't talk to you openly; they don't seem to talk to others easily.
..............................**GANNO & MALIHA**, *REFUGE*

Difficult circumstances ....

On Mondays I come to the Cowley Club where I get help with my English and where I meet lots of other people, all foreigners living in difficult circumstances. I have found it a real comfort to meet others who are in similar positions to myself.

Most days I go straight to the library in Brighton. I spend a lot of time reading, mainly newspapers, in English and Turkish. I try to keep up with the news from my country. I love reading. The library also provides free Internet access, which is wonderful.
....**HASAN**, *REFUGE*

Escape ....

On the surface I appear to be as well as anyone could under this pressure. But no one can see what is going on inside me. How can I convey the torture of hearing my child on the phone say,

COMMUNITY

"I just want to cuddle you. Why won't you let me?" Sometimes when he speaks to me he cries and says, "This is enough Daddy, please, just come back!" This is the worst thing for a parent – a child's request that is impossible to fulfil. For a normal parent it would be so easy, but I can't respond. Can you imagine the pain of not being able touch him or comfort him?

I fled my country to escape prison, to stay alive and to keep my family safe but, for the last two years, I have been a prisoner here. My wife and my son are in Iran, where they also are, in their own way, prisoners. In this beautiful, green prison called the UK, I have learnt that it is not just walls and bars that keep you in chains.

.... **A.N.**, *REFUGE*

> **'I have been a prisoner here'**

Angels

If there weren't so many angelic people around me I, like so many hundreds of other 'failed' asylum seekers, would be sleeping on people's floors or in night shelters or sleeping rough on park benches and begging for food. But I have survived with the help of the people here who look after me. They are like angels; more than angels – I can't find words that do them justice. They live the words Human Rights; they put their own comfort second and do so without hesitation or any consideration of their own positions.

.... **A.N.**, *REFUGE*

CHAPTER 6

Mr and Mrs Cowley

Harry & Harriet Cowley, *Who Was Harry Cowley?* QueenSpark Books.

Harry's Legacy

Bread of Heaven..............................

Five hundred people packed St. Peter's Church. Many hundreds more waited outside in the cold. A local television audience watched the service at home. March 11, 1971, and Brighton was paying its last respects to Harry Cowley, 'The Guv'nor'.

His body had lain in state at St. Peter's overnight, and now a huge wreath of yellow chrysanthemums woven into the shape of a bowler hat lay on the coffin, alongside a set of chimney sweep's brushes. The congregation sang Harry's favourite hymn, *Bread of Heaven*.

Then the funeral procession moved slowly to Brighton and Preston Cemetery, detouring up Trafalgar Street and across into Upper Gardner Street, through Harry's old market-trading haunts.

Who was this Brighton chimney sweep who wore a bowler hat? What had he done to become a local folk hero? More than a decade later, we asked people in the streets of Brighton, "Who was Harry Cowley?" One of those names you've heard.

The chap they used to call The Guv'nor. He used to knock a bit of money off his sweeping to help old-age pensioners. He was always for the down and outs, and if there was a place empty he would try to get them in. He was a rough diamond. He should have been Mayor of Brighton. He didn't have any political side to him. He was an independent man. He was a socialist rebel without knowing what the socialist cause is. He took the blows and stood out all through his life.

> **'He was always for the down and outs'**

Harry Cowley's name also cropped up in almost every life story sent into the community writing and publishing group, QueenSpark. That's how we decided to make a book of Harry's extraordinary life. We gathered newspaper clippings covering a fifty-year span, and discovered old family scrapbooks and photo albums. None of our work team had actually known Harry Cowley, so we interviewed family and friends, neighbours, workmates, and people who had battled with Harry, and sometimes against him.
.... *WHO WAS HARRY COWLEY?*

Harry Cowley, Chimney Sweep, *Who Was Harry Cowley?* **QueenSpark Books.**

For a Cause

Natural Orator ....
"I came back from France thinking I was going to be alright for a job, but it was worse than ever. You knew if you was used to work you couldn't keep going to the Labour Exchange." Harry Cowley and thousands of other ex-servicemen were rewarded for their war service with useless decorations and unemployment. This desperate state of affairs became Harry's first cause. He revealed himself a born leader and a natural orator: "Outside the old Exchange there was a sand bin. So I got on it and addressed

the boys. It was the first time in my life I ever got on a platform. I was so fed up with coming back and no work."

He addressed the unemployed men with fierce determination: "Well now boys, it's no good of us messing about with the Labour Exchange. Let's go where we can get a job. There's only one place we can go in this town and that's down the Town Hall. I'll go down and I want you to come with me." Confronted by the police for disturbing the peace, Harry cheekily replied, "They're nothing to do with me. They're following me about."

Harry won this first battle with the authorities. He secured work for 600 men on the widening of Ditchling Road. But he was not

Unemployed workers outside Brighton Labour Exchange, Western Road, Brighton, 1939. Royal Pavilion & Museums.

happy when he discovered that 'his boys' were receiving below the union rate: "I said, 'Well down tools boys, and straight down to the Town Hall.' I went before the Council and put the case and got the trade union rate."

A men's unemployed centre in Tichborne Street was one successful result of these protests. The club gave unemployed men a respectability that they were fast losing as the vacant days crept by. They organized lively campaigning marches, where banners were waved and bugles blown.

Despite the high unemployment rate, these men were accused of being unskilled and lazy. When a Brighton councillor announced, "Harry Cowley is the leader of a bunch of unemployables," Harry and 'his boys' set out to prove him wrong by marching along the Sussex coast looking for work. Day after day the column of unemployed tramped from one Sussex town to the next. By day they badgered employers, at night they slept in barns and sheds.

After a couple of weeks they were back in Brighton ... "Now," said Harry, "you dare call us unemployables again."
.... *WHO WAS HARRY COWLEY?*

2,000 loaves a week..........................

The men also spent a lot of time collecting money and food for unemployed families. Harry was distributing more than 2,000 loaves a week and churn after churn of milk. He ran boxing in the Dome and concerts at the Grand Theatre, to pay for meat and groceries and first-off boots for the children.

The Town Council was frightened by Harry Cowley's constant protests. To quieten him down they bought him a set of

chimney sweep tools. But Harry had the last laugh. When the unemployed or any other cause needed leadership he dropped his brushes and reached for his drums.
.... *WHO WAS HARRY COWLEY?*

Labour Man

Tireless Work ....
Everyone who knew Harry tells a story of The Guv'nor's tireless work in the neighbourhood. They remember Harry organizing outings for the poor kids of Southover St., finding furniture for old people moved in a slum clearance, or standing up to the Board of Guardians to get more money for an out-of-luck family.

Mrs Williams was a neighbour of the Cowleys: "Anything you wanted, go to Mr Cowley, he'd help you, if you was in trouble, no matter what trouble. Probably hadn't got the money himself, but he'd find something to help them with. He used to have big concerts and do all this, that and the other so little kiddies could have a good Christmas. He'd give the old people 10s notes, pound notes; what he thought they most needed. And then, when the children was in want of any boots or shoes, if the authorities wouldn't give it to them, Harry Cowley got round. I remember my dad when he had nothing, he come to us and give us all shoes, and there was eight of us."

These bread-and-butter needs were the core of Harry Cowley's politics. His organized campaigns for the unemployed and for better housing were simply an extension of this determination to improve the lives of his working-class neighbours.
.... *WHO WAS HARRY COWLEY?*

It don't come right to me ....

This was Harry Cowley's rallying cry. If he believed something wasn't right he would fight to change it. But what shaped his strong opinions on such a variety of issues? What persuaded him to take up a fight?

According to Ruby Weston, "He wasn't for the people who'd got business or got money." And he wasn't for rules or rulers. As Labour man Stan Fitch recalls, "He could not be controlled by rules – he challenged authority and defied it openly."

Harry was for the 'underdog', for working-class people in hard times: "He was a real Labour man – he must have been because he was for the working class." (Ruby Weston)

Sometimes those he tried to help could not immediately see how he was trying to help them...

As Ernie Scrase reflects, Harry was for people rather than political parties: "Harry was not representing people, he was trying to help them. He had no practical political ambitions, I don't think he had any ambitions for self-glorification at all. It was just an honest desire to help people who were, in his opinion, more down-trodden than he was."
.... *WHO WAS HARRY COWLEY?*

> '**He was a real Labour Man ... he was for the working class**'

If Harry Cowley was alive today ....

"He would be fighting for the people that had nowhere to live, he would be fighting for the people that had nothing. He would most definitely be fighting against the cuts in the social services, and he would most definitely not be in agreement with the three political parties today. I think as a great individualist he would have probably tried to form

some organization of his own, even though it was a local organization."
.... *WHO WAS HARRY COWLEY?*

Harriet Cowley

Harriet Cowley, *Who Was Harry Cowley?* QueenSpark Books.

My mother ....
"If it hadn't been for my mother, my father wouldn't have got anywhere."
.... RUBY LUCAS, *WHO WAS HARRY COWLEY?*

Soldiering on...............
You would not have seen Harriet Cowley rallying the crowds at The Level, or leading the unemployed.

Maybe if you had been observant you could have spotted her organising an O.A.P. party, or clearing the debris at a vacant house.

'The wives of working-class heroes rarely receive the applause they deserve'

The wives of working-class heroes rarely receive the applause they deserve. Out of the limelight, it is the women who are steadily soldiering on, with an endurance that men might find impossible. As their daughter, Ruby Lucas, points out, Harry would have been no-one without the help and support of Harriet.

One reason that Harriet could not play the same public role as Harry was her lack of free time. Harriet was very hard-working and rarely had a minute free. She worked a twelve-hour day, balancing her paid laundry work with her unpaid housework,

plus a multitude of other tasks. The house of a chimney sweep was never easy to keep clean. A neighbour Mrs Humphries remembers, "When you went down to his house all you could smell was the soot and the black, it was the chimney dust."
.... *WHO WAS HARRY COWLEY?*

Make ends meet ....

It was also a daily struggle for Harriet to make ends meet. The Cowley family was never well-to-do. In the early days when the children were young, they lived on a frugal diet of bread and jam and stews. Yet as the youngest son, Abe Cowley, is quick to point out, "We never wanted for anything," and Harriet kept smiling through thick and thin. Mrs Humphries recalls, "She used to go up to the laundry and sing...oh she did used to sing."

Working-class politics was regarded as a 'man's world'; The Guv'nor was surrounded by his 'boys'. In spite of this prejudice and the long hours she worked Harriet still managed to involve herself in community politics. She had her own firm beliefs. In the words of Abe Cowley, "She was the sort of person who if she saw a kid walking up the street with a hole in their shoes, she would give them the money to go and buy another pair." She participated in Vigilante meetings, and was one of the main workers at old-age pensioner events.

"It's been a bit worrying you know. Still I stuck it and I thought he was doing something good for other people. P'r'aps what I couldn't do, and why hinder him in what he wanted to do in the way of goodness."

It is not surprising that their relationship 'had its ups and downs'. At times Harry's outside involvement put pressure on the marriage. "Well I sometimes feel I want to give up, so he

'In spite of this prejudice ... Harriet still managed to involve herself in community politics'

*Who Was
Harry Cowley?*
QueenSpark Books.

says, 'don't be like that, we carry on you and me,' so we do."
In spite of the rows they had, which were mainly over other
people, they retained a romantic view of each other. "I don't
know about being married to a rebel but I've enjoyed every
minute of it," and Harry's belief was, "We married for love, and
that's why it worked."

.... *WHO WAS HARRY COWLEY?*